PRAYERS

that change things in your

RELATIONSHIPS

PRAYERS
that change things in your
RELATIONSHIPS

LLOYD HILDEBRAND

BRIDGE
LOGOS

Alachua, Florida 32615

Bridge-Logos

Alachua, FL 32615 USA

Prayers That Change Things In Your Relationships
by Lloyd Hildebrand

Copyright ©2012 by Lloyd Hildebrand

Printed in the United States of America.

Library of Congress Catalog Card Number:
  2013932315

International Standard Book Number:
  978-0-88270-012-0

Unless otherwise noted, all Scripture quotations are
from the King James Version of the Holy Bible.

VP 02-11-13

DEDICATION

TO MY SWEETHEART, Peggy Hildebrand. My relationship with her has lasted for more than forty-two years, and she has brought such wonderful happiness, joy, and contentment to me. Peggy, I love you with all my heart, and I look forward to the next forty-two years. May God bless you in everything you set your mind to do. You are a true blessing to me, our children, grandchildren, and so many others. Thank you for always being there for me.

CONTENTS

PART III—FRUITFUL PRAYERS THAT CHANGE THINGS IN ALL YOUR RELATIONSHIPS— THESE PRAYERS ARE BASED ON THE FRUIT OF THE SPRIT

(See Galatians 5:5:22-23.)

PART IV—PRAYERS THAT CHANGE THINGS IN YOUR FAMILY RELATIONSHIPS

PART V—PRAYERS THAT CHANGE THINGS IN YOUR CHURCH RELATIONSHIPS

PART VI—PRAYERS THAT CHANGE YOUR RELATIONSHIP WITH YOURSELF

PART VII—PRAYERS THAT CHANGE THINGS IN YOUR COMMUNITY AND WORK RELATIONSHIPS

PART VIII—BIBLE BLESSINGS FOR YOUR RELATIONSHIPS

INTRODUCTION

PRAYER helps us build our relationships, and relationships are so important in our lives. In fact, they are the part of our lives that will live on forever, because love never dies. What we invest in our relationships now will pay dividends forever.

The prayers of this book incorporate biblical principles and promises to help you build your relationships with God, family members, friends, co-workers, neighbors, fellow-believers, yourself, and others.

Sometimes things need to be changed in our relationships, and prayer can be the facilitator for bringing about those changes. The prayers within this book will help you to discover ways to change things in your various relationships, because they will help you to see what God's will is for each relationship. The goal of each prayer is to foster healthy, happy, and effective relationships in your life.

When you come right down to it, relationships are the most important things in life, and because they are, we must cultivate them with great care. Someone has said that the only thing that will count for eternity is what we've done for others, especially family members.

I remember when a friend of mine was diagnosed with terminal cancer in her early forties. I asked her, "What would you do if you knew you were going to die today?" Her answer was simple and profound, "I would go home, sit on my couch, and hold my two sons very close to me."

In the face of losing everything, this young woman realized that relationships are the only things that really count. Paul put it this way, "The only thing that counts is faith expressing itself through love" (Galatians 5:6, NIV).

This truth is expressed in this little poem: "Only one life will soon be past; only what's done for Christ will last." We need to invest our time and our energies into those things that have lasting power—relationships.

We're all familiar with the saying, "The family that prays together stays together." The prayers in this book can be used by families in their devotions, and this will result in greater cohesiveness within the family unit. They may be used by individuals, as well, and this will help them see what God wants them to do in order to bring change into their relationships.

This is a very true saying also: "It's impossible to hate someone you are praying for." Prayer is an essential ingredient in strengthening all the relationships in your life. This, along with the Word of God, is a mixture that yields tremendous power.

Would you like to have better relationships with your parents, spouse, children, co-workers, fellow church members, neighbors, pastor, yourself, and others? Take the prayers in this book very seriously, for they will help you while providing effective intercession for them.

Two of the foundational ingredients for building an effective relationship are love and trust. The first two chapters of this book deal with these vital topics. Part I—Components of an Effective Relationship— contains teaching that is based primarily on the fruit of the Spirit. (See Galatians 5:22-23.) These fruit are core dimensions in building all effective relationships and they will lead you to become a very fruitful Christian, as you bear the fruit of the Spirit in all the relationships and responsibilities of your life.

My prayer for you, dear reader, is: "{May the} God of our Lord Jesus Christ, the Father of glory, . . .give unto you the spirit of wisdom and revelation in the knowledge of him: the eyes of your understanding being enlightened; that ye may know what is the hope of his calling, and what the riches of the glory of his inheritance in the saints {is}, and what is the exceeding greatness of his power to us-ward who believe, according to the working of his mighty power" (Ephesians 1:17-19).

PART I

COMPONENTS OF AN EFFECTIVE RELATIONSHIP

Chapter 1

LOVE—A KEY COMPONENT IN ALL YOUR RELATIONSHIPS

ONE of my favorite scriptural passages says, "Beloved, let us love one another: for love is of God; and every one that loveth is born of God, and knoweth God. He that loveth not knoweth not God; for God is love" (1 John 4:7–8).

We must love because God is love. Ponder that simple statement for a moment. Because this is true, we can say with certainty:

- When we are moving in love, we are moving in God.
- Love comes from God.
- God is love, and love is a manifestation of God.

Love is the first fruit listed by Paul in the fruit of the Spirit. He writes, "But the fruit of the Spirit is love, joy, peace, longsuffering, gentleness, goodness, faith, meekness, temperance; against such there is no law" (Galatians 5:22–23). These are nine luscious fruits that we are to bear in all the relationships and responsibilities of our lives. We don't have to produce these fruit, because they are already there. Our job is to simply let them come forth so that others will be able to

7

taste and see that the Lord is good. (See Psalm 34:8.)

I like what Dwight L. Moody wrote about the fruit of the Spirit: "The fruit of the Spirit begins with love. There are nine graces spoken of, and of these nine Paul puts love at the head of the list; love is the first thing, the first thing in that precious cluster of fruit. Someone has said that all the other eight can be put in terms of love. Joy is love exulting; peace is love in repose; longsuffering is love on trial; gentleness is love in society; goodness is love in action; faith is love on the battlefield; meekness is love at school; and temperance is love in training. So it is love all the way; love at the top, love at the bottom, and all the way along down this list of graces. If we only just brought forth the fruit of the Spirit, what a world we would have! Men would have no desire to do evil."

How true this is! Imagine a world in which the fruit of the Spirit abound. That's what Heaven is like, and in Heaven with its atmosphere of love there will be no war, disease, death, evil, terrorism, or sin. The opposites of these fruit are hatred, misery, unsettledness, anger, pride, evil, doubt, and a life that is out of control.

We need to learn to submit to the Holy Spirit in order to live a life that is above all fleshy lusts. These differing qualities help us to distinguish between the Kingdom of God (where we can live daily) and the kingdom of this world, which is filled with darkness and evil.

We must remember that we are citizens of the Kingdom of God, not the kingdom of this world. We live by a different law than the rest of society, and that law is love. Therefore, let us walk in love toward all. By so doing, we will be known to be the Disciples of Christ, for love is the mark of every disciple, as Jesus pointed out.

We are able to love because God first loved us. The Bible says, "We love him, because he first loved us" (1 John 4:19). This goes along with the truth that God is love. As Jesus said, "Without me ye can do nothing" (John 15:5). Certainly something as important and powerful as love cannot be accomplished without Him, but through Him we can do all things, including loving others and ourselves. (See Philippians 4:13.)

The Supreme Commandment is: "Jesus said unto him, Thou shalt love the Lord thy God with all thy heart, and with all they soul, and with all thy mind. This is the first and great commandment. And the second is like unto it, Thou shalt love thy neighbor as thyself" (Matthew 22:37-39).

God would not give us a commandment like this if we were unable to follow it. He expects us to heed the first and great commandment and to obey the second one, as well.

Mother Teresa wrote, "Thou shalt love the Lord thy God with thy whole heart, with thy whole soul and with thy whole mind. This is the commandment of the great God, and He cannot command the impossible. Love is a fruit in season at all times, and within the reach of every hand. Anyone may gather it and no limit is set."

The fruit of love is always fresh and pleasant. Therefore, our prayer should be, "Help me to bear the fruit of love in all the relationships and responsibilities of my life."

Love is the bond of perfection—"And above all these things put on charity [love], which is the bond of perfectness" (Colossians 3:14). Love is the glue that takes the pieces of our fragmented lives and relationships and puts them back together in a perfectly cohesive whole.

There can be no perfection or wholeness or completion in our lives without love. We need to love and be loved, for this will lead to wholeness (and holiness) in our lives.

Love is far more than just a feeling. It is a commitment to those we care about. It is a choice we make. After we set our wills in the direction of love, we can expect the feeling of love to follow. Rainer Maria Rilke wrote, "This is the miracle that happens every time to those who really love: the more they give, the more they possess of that precious, nourishing love from which flowers and children have their strength and which could help all human beings if they would take it without doubting."

Love is the strongest force in the world. It is even stronger than death. There is no fear in love, for perfect loves casts out all fear. (See 1 John 4:18.) If we have fear, we have not been made perfect in love. Love is a giant eraser that wipes away any feelings of fear and anxiety.

We must love God, others, and ourselves. Dr. Martin

Luther King wrote, "What then is the conclusion of the matter? Love yourself, if that means rational and healthy self-interest. You are commanded to do that. That is the length of life. Love your neighbor as you love yourself. You are commanded to do that. That is the breadth of life. But never forget that there is a first and even greater commandment: 'Love the Lord thy God with all thy heart, and with all thy soul, and with all thy mind.' This is the height of life. Only by a painstaking development of all three of these dimensions can you expect to live a complete life."

The Bible says: "That Christ may dwell in your hearts by faith; that ye, being rooted and grounded in love, may be able to comprehend with all saints what is the breadth, and length, and depth, and height; and to know the love of Christ, which passeth knowledge, that ye might be filled with all the fulness of God" (Ephesians 3:17-19).

Such love is a grace that is given to us. For many of us it was this love of God that attracted us to Jesus in the first place. He is our first love, and we never want to lose that relationship. "But God commendeth his love toward us, in that, while we were yet sinners, Christ died for us" (Romans 5:8).

This amazing love goes beyond human understanding. "For God so loved the world, that he gave his only begotten Son, that whosoever believeth in him should not perish, but have everlasting life" (John 3:16). The first response of love is always to give and give and give. That's the way the Father and Jesus love us—they gave so much for us. And this love demands that we give love and service in return.

"For unto whomsoever much is given, of him shall be much required" (Luke 12:48). God's love for us has given us so much, and we must realize that everything we are and have comes from Him. His love compels us to love others and ourselves.

What amazing love! What are its marvelous effects in our lives? Thomas Kempis writes, "Love is a great and good thing, and alone makes heavy burdens light and bears in equal balance things pleasing and things displeasing. Love bears a heavy burden and does not feel it, and love makes bitter things tasteful and sweet. The noble love of Jesus perfectly imprinted in man's soul makes a man do great things, and stirs him always to desire perfection and to grow more and more in grace and goodness.

"Love knows no measure, but is fervent without measure. It feels no burden; it regards no labor; it desires more than it can obtain. It complains of no impossibility, for it thinks all things that can be done for its Beloved are possible and lawful. So, love does many great things and brings them to completion—things in which he who is no lover faints and fails.

"Love wakes much and sleeps little and, in sleeping, does not sleep. It faints and is not weary; it is restricted in its liberty and is in great freedom. It sees reasons to fear and does not fear, but, like an ember or a spark of fire, flames always upward, by the fervor of its love, toward God, and through the special help of grace is delivered from all perils and dangers" (Thomas Kempis).

Be filled with the love of God that His love would overflow through you and course its way to others. May the love of God pour forth from our lives in an ever-stronger flow, that people would be attracted to God who is love. Then, as our love builds within the Church, may it become a powerful tsunami that gathers people into its dynamic flow.

As you pray the prayers within this book, may your heart be filled with love. "That Christ may dwell in your hearts by faith; that ye, being rooted and grounded in love, may be able to comprehend with all saints what is the breadth, and length, and depth, and height; and to know the love of Christ, which passeth knowledge, that ye might be filled with all the fullness of God" (Ephesians 3:17-19).

Love is unconditional positive regard, and this absolutely must be a part of every relationship or else it will not be a relationship at all.

Chapter 2

TRUST—A QUALITY THAT UNDERGIRDS YOUR RELATIONSHIPS

TRUST is a firm belief or confidence in the honesty, trustworthiness, integrity, reliability, genuineness, and love of another person. It entails faith and reliance.

We must trust God, those we love, and ourselves if our relationships are to have any meaning and longevity.

Another one of my favorite Bible passages is "Trust in the Lord with all thine heart; and lean not unto thine own understanding. In all thy ways acknowledge him, and he shall direct thy paths" (Proverbs 3:5-6).

We are to love God with all our heart and we are to trust Him with all our heart as well. Our relationship with Him is based on these key components and the same should be true in all our other relationships, including our relationship with ourselves.

Even business relationships are maintained by trust.

I like the attitude that was expressed by Job: "Though he slay me, yet will I trust in him" (Job 13:15).

It is difficult to restore trust once it is broken. Someone has said, "Trust is like a vase...once it's broken, though you can fix it, the vase will never be the same again."

Because David fully trusted in the Lord, he was able to pray, "Cause me to hear thy lovingkindness in the morning; for in thee do I trust: cause we to know the way wherein I should walk; for I lift up my soul unto thee" (Psalm 143:8).

Trusting the Lord leads to deep inner peace, as Isaiah said, "Thou wilt keep him in perfect peace whose mind is stayed on thee: because he trusteth in thee. Trust ye in the Lord forever: for in the Lord Jehovah is everlasting strength" (Isaiah 26:3-4).

Follow your heart and learn to trust your heart, for it is the organ of love within your body. It is true that, as Walter Anderson wrote, "We're never so vulnerable than when we trust someone—but paradoxically, if we cannot trust, neither can we find love or joy." Trust God and trust yourself.

Both love and trust are investments that make us vulnerable to hurt, but it is a good investment nonetheless, because it is rewarding to both you and the other person.

When it comes to trusting others, we all know that this can be difficult at times. Hurts from the past tend to make us cautious when it comes to trusting others. Prayer is very helpful when it comes to this. Prayer helps us to see beyond the circumstances, into the spiritual dimension, and this always changes our perspective.

Prayer helps us to see into the hearts of those we pray about and desire to trust. It opens windows of understanding that lead to a deeper sense of love and trust and to a commitment that nothing can shatter.

Prayer helps us to forgive.

Paul gives us great advice regarding all relationships when he writes, "Let all bitterness, and wrath, and anger, and clamour, and evil speaking, be put away from you, with all malice: and be ye kind one to another, tenderhearted, forgiving one another, even as God for Christ's sake hath forgiven you" (Ephesians 4:31-32

Forgiveness is the key to relationships that need trust restored. We need to forgive those who wrong us so that we can be free to love and trust those who have hurt us. Prayer is the only thing that makes this possible.

The following two verses are clear in showing us that we can be secure in the love of God as we learn to trust Him in all things: "For I am persuaded, that neither death, nor life, nor angels, nor principalities, nor powers, nor things present, nor things to come, nor height, nor depth, nor any other creature, shall be able to separate us from the love of God, which is in Christ Jesus our Lord" (Romans 8:38-39).

As you pray the prayers within this book, you will learn a new way of trusting God, others, and yourself. "For the Lord our God is a sun and shield: the Lord will give grace and glory: no good thing will he withhold from them that walk uprightly. O Lord of hosts, blessed is the man that trusteth in thee" (Psalm 84:11-12).

Chapter 3

JOY—WARMTH IN YOUR RELATIONSHIPS

JOY is a necessary part of any relationship because it provides a feeling of warmth and comfort to everyone involved. It is deeper than happiness and far deeper than any other Christian virtue. Listen to the words of Samuel Dickey Gordon: "Joy is a distinctly Christian word and a Christian thing. It is the reverse of happiness. Happiness is the result of what happens of an agreeable sort. Joy has its springs deep down inside. And that spring never runs dry, no matter what happens. Only Jesus gives that joy. He had joy, singing its music within, even under the shadow of the Cross. It is an unknown word and thing except as He has sway within."

Joy—a distinctly Christian word and thing. Joy—a spring that never runs dry. Joy—an unknown word and thing unless Jesus is the center of our lives.

"The joy of the Lord is your strength" (Nehemiah 8:10). It is our strength because it will not let any form of discouragement, anxiety, or doubt enter our lives.

Out of the wellspring of joy relationships in our lives are greatly strengthened, as well. Simply put, joy makes people feel comfortable and accepted. It brings forth smiles and laughter. It seasons our relationships with good feelings and childlike wonder.

Jesus said, "Except ye be converted, and become as little children, ye shall not enter into the kingdom of heaven" (Matthew 18:3). Childlikeness is a quality that few seem to possess. A childlike person is humble, curious, open to all life has to offer, forgiving, trusting, and innocent. These are wonderful qualities, and they become possible to us as adults as we learn to walk in joy.

Joy can transform the sadness of another into gladness. This Hasidic quote from Bernard Mandelbaum's *Choose Life* says it well: "When people are merry and dance, it sometimes happens that they catch hold of someone who is sitting outside and grieving, pull him into the round, and make him rejoice with them. The same happens in the heart of one who rejoices: grief and sorrow draw away from him, but it is a special virtue to pursue them with courage and to draw grief into gladness, so that all the strength of sorrow may be transformed into joy."

Let the fruit of joy season all your relationships, and then you will see miracles taking place in your life and the lives of others.

"Rejoice with them that do rejoice, and weep with them that weep" (Romans 12:15). Here Paul is talking about the quality of empathy that enables us to feel what another person feels. To rejoice with those who are rejoicing is a blessing to both you and them.

In Proverbs we read, "A merry heart doeth good, like a medicine" (Proverbs 17:22). This is a medicine that we can share with others.

As you pray the prayers within this book, may you experience the fullness of the joy of the Lord so that you will be able to share His abiding joy with everyone.

"For the kingdom of God is not meat and drink; but righteousness, and peace, and joy in the Holy Ghost" (Romans 14:17).

Rejoice evermore.

Chapter 4

PEACE—A QUALITY THAT SURPASSES ALL UNDERSTANDING

NOTICE how the Apostle Paul weaves prayer together with peace: "Be careful for nothing; but in everything by prayer and supplication with thanksgiving let your requests be made known unto God. And the peace of God, which passeth all understanding, shall keep your hearts and minds through Christ Jesus" (Philippians 4:6-7).

May peace be with you as you continue to read and as you pray the prayers within this book. "God has called us to peace" (1 Corinthians 7:15). He wants us to live peaceably with everyone. (See Romans 12:18.)

I like what Mother Teresa had to say about peace: "Let us not use bombs and guns to overcome the world. Let us use love and compassion. Peace begins with a smile—smile five times a day at someone you don't really want to smile at—do it for peace. So let us radiate the peace of God and so light His light and extinguish in the world and in the hearts of all men all hatred and love for power."

Peace in our lives and in our prayers will bring about

peace in the world, one person at a time. It will change all our relationships because it is contagious. As you learn to radiate peace in your relationships with others, they will change, your relationships will change, and you will change. Greater peace will begin to fill the environment.

Inner peace causes us to become peacemakers and this, as John Stott pointed out, ". . . is a divine work. For peace means reconciliation, and God is the author of peace and reconciliation . . . It is hardly surprising, therefore, that the particular blessing which attaches to peacemakers is that 'they shall be called sons of God.' For they are seeking to do what their Father has done, loving people with His love. . . .It is the devil who is a troublemaker; it is God who loves reconciliation and who now through His children, as formerly through His only begotten Son, is bent on making peace."

Are you a peacemaker? If you are, you are a true child of God.

There is no anxiety in peace. There is no turmoil, anger, or fear in peace. Peace is a bridge between people. When you learn to come from peace in all your relationships visual changes will take place. It simply cannot be otherwise, for peace brings people together.

Let peace rule in your life, that nothing would ever be able to disturb you. Lloyd John Ogilvie wrote, "Peace is the result of grace. It literally means, 'to bind together.' In other words, the peace which comes from unmerited, unearned love can weave and bind our fragmented lives into wholeness. And the civil war of divergent drives, which makes us feel like rubber bands stretched in all directions, is ended. He is in charge of now, and shows the way for each new day."

Similarly, God's peace can weave and bind fragmented relationships together.

Peace in your heart is a sign of reconciliation with God and that very peace will lead you to be reconciled with others. St. Francis of Assisi wrote:

> "Lord, make me an instrument of your peace;
> Where there is hatred, let me sow love;
> Where there is injury, pardon;
> Where there is doubt, faith;
> Where there is despair, hope;
> Where there is darkness, light;
> Where there is sadness, joy.
> O Divine Master,
> Grant that I may not so much seek
> To be consoled, as to console;
> To be understood, as to understand;
> To be loved, as to love.
> For it is in giving that we receive;
> It is in pardoning that we are pardoned;
> It is in dying that we are born to eternal life."

Now that's a prayer that changes the way we think about life and all our relationships, isn't it?

Chapter 5

PATIENCE—AN ATTRIBUTE OF MATURE RELATIONSHIPS

IT has been said, "Patience is a virtue. Possess it if you can. Seldom found in women. Never found in man!" Though I'm not at all sure that this statement is entirely accurate, it does point to the fact that patience is a difficult virtue to acquire, no matter what your gender is. Nonetheless, it is a fruit of the Holy Spirit, and if He lives within you, it is entirely possible for you to become a patient person in your relationships, for He is patient with us.

As you know, patience sometimes involves waiting. Paul writes, "Love is patient" (1 Corinthians 13:4, NIV). Here is what Billy Graham has to say about the value of patience in relationships: "Patience is the transcendent radiance of a loving and tender heart which, in its dealings with those around it, looks kindly and graciously upon them. Patience graciously, compassionately, and with understanding judges the faults of others without unjust criticism. Patience also includes perseverance—the ability to bear up under weariness, strain, and persecution when doing the work of the Lord."

We need to be patient with God, others, and ourselves.

Evelyn Underhill writes, "Patience with ourselves is a duty for Christians and the only real humility. For it means patience with a growing creature whom God has taken in hand and whose completion He will effect in His own time and His own way. 'Rest in the Lord, wait patiently on Him and He shall give thee thy heart's desire.'"

Yes, you must learn to be patient with yourself.

When you are patient with another person, you learn to listen to them and to the feelings that lie behind their words. Love is patient; it is also ". . . kind. It does not envy, it does not boast, it is not proud. It is not rude, it is not self-seeking, it is not easily angered, it keeps no record of wrongs" (1 Corinthians 13:4–5 NIV).

As we enter into relationships with others, patience plays a vital role, for it shows respect, humility, and peace, all of which are keys to an effective relationship. Patience involves a commitment that promises to endure, no matter what the circumstances may be. Patience is resilient and it perseveres through every difficulty without getting annoyed or agitated with the other person.

When a couple exchanges wedding vows, they frequently promise to each other that they will remain true to each other ". . . for richer, for poorer, in sickness and in health, until death us do part." This vow forms a covenant relationship in the sight of God, and it is inviolable if both parties remain totally committed to each other.

This vow requires them to be patient with each other.

This kind of commitment is important in all relationships. It is a commitment to helping the other person attain to the very best in all that they do. It is a commitment to a lasting relationship no matter what may happen.

Remember, commitment is a choice you make to engage in a relationship that you will protect and preserve at all costs. We may say, "Please be patient with me; God is not finished with me yet," and this is an appropriate thing to say. In saying this, though, we must remember that the same thing applies to the other person.

Leonardo da Vinci wrote, "So in like manner you must grow in patience when you meet with great wrongs, and they will then be powerless to vex your mind."

James writes, "Knowing this, that the trying of your faith worketh patience. But let patience have her perfect work, that ye may be perfect and entire, wanting nothing" (James 1:3-4).

Let patience have her perfect work in your life and your relationships. This will bring wholeness, healing, and abundance into your relationships. It will change your life.

Chapter 6

KINDNESS—A RESPECTFUL ATTITUDE

"PUT on therefore, as the elect of God, holy and beloved, bowels of mercies, *kindness*, humbleness of mind, meekness, longsuffering; forbearing one another and forgiving one another" (Colossians 3:12-13, italics mine).

Kindness may seem to be a rare behavior in today's society. It is a quality of being considerate and respectful toward others. Kindness seeks good for another person.

I agree with Lloyd John Ogilvie that "Kindness is a sign of greatness." It certainly does not have any weakness in it whatsoever. It is gentle, though. The kind of greatness that comes from kindness is a very desirable goal.

Speaking of the strength and greatness of kindness, Charles H. Spurgeon writes, "Kind words bring no blisters on the tongue that speaks them. Kind words are never wasted. Like scattered seeds, they spring up in unexpected places. Kindness is a conquering weapon. Kindness should not be all on one side. One good turn must have another as its return, or it will not be fair.

He who expects kindness should show kindness."

Expressing kindness in words and deeds is not a challenging endeavor. It can be done with simplicity and grace. It makes you feel good when you are kind, and it goes without saying that it makes the recipient of the kindness feel good as well.

Kindness involves so many things, including forgiveness, service, words, humility, friendship, leadership, compassion, encouragement, cheerfulness, receiving, giving, sacrifice, and respect. It is an important virtue indeed. It is an attitude that, when practiced, becomes second nature.

This truly is greatness, and it is this kind of greatness that we want to bring into every relationship in our lives. Love is kind. Colin Urquhart gives us these words from the Master: "Instead of being easily roused to anger, I am merciful, patient, loving, and kind. Because my love lives in you, don't be easily angered either, even when people do foolish things."

A recent movie was entitled, "Pay It Forward," and this suggests that when someone does a good deed for us, we should respond by passing it on and doing a good deed for others. During a recent holiday season, people demonstrated great kindness by going to the layaway departments in stores and anonymously paying for items that others had put on layaway. This is true kindness, and it does not seek a reward or any recognition.

Let's forge a chain of kindness that reaches around the world by doing good deeds whenever we can. The links of that chain begin to be formed as we are kind to those we love first. Then we will keep extending the chain by reaching out to others.

Let me challenge you with this idea: find someone who doesn't seem to like you. Try to figure out a way in which you can be kind to that person. I think you will discover that interpersonal kindness has the power to change that relationship forever.

Any random act of kindness is not easily forgotten. It is easy to recall when others have been kind to us. These are sweet memories indeed.

Peter wrote, "Giving all diligence, add to your faith virtue; and to virtue knowledge; and to knowledge temperance; and to temperance patience; and to patience godliness; *and to godliness brother kindness*; and to brotherly kindness charity" (2 Peter 1:5-7, italics mine).

Chapter 7

GOODNESS—A GODLIKE QUALITY

ALL goodness comes from God, and there is a sense in which goodness and godliness mean the same thing. Simply stated, goodness is love in action.

Take a few minutes to read the Sermon on the Mount. It is a complete recipe for goodness in our relationships. It speaks of gentleness, mercy, purity of heart, making peace, and how to respond to persecution.

Jesus said, "Love your enemies, and pray for those who persecute you in order that you may be sons of your Father in heaven" (Matthew 4:44-45, NASB). This is being good in the face of wickedness. Yes, it is possible to be good even to evil-doers.

Goodness involves generosity, giving, and a total lack of selfishness. John Wesley gave us good advice:

"Do all the good you can, by all the means you can, in all the ways you can, in all the places you can, at all the times you can, to all the people you can, as long as ever you can."

God living within you is the source of any goodness you possess and act upon. Thoreau wrote, "Goodness is the only investment that never fails."

We can invest goodness in the lives of those around us, even perfect strangers, and we should see immediate results if only a smile or a thank you. Such responses go a long way in helping us to know that we have done something good for someone.

This does not mean, however, that we should be good in order to receive rewards. They are simply a by-product of goodness. C.H. Spurgeon wrote, "Nothing is a good work unless it is done with a good motive; and there is no motive which can be said to be good but for the glory of God. He who performs good works with a view to save himself, does not do them from a good motive, because his motive is selfish. He who does them also to gain the esteem of his fellows and for the good of society has a laudable motive. What end had we in view? If for the benefit of our fellow-creatures, then let our fellow-creatures pay us; but that has nought to do with God."

Even at work, though, whatever our work may be, we need to exhibit an attitude of goodness that is willing to go above and beyond what is expected of us.

Instead of trying to be good, let God make you good. Rather, let Him fill you with His goodness so that you will become His goodness in the world. C.S. Lewis wrote, "The Christian is in a different position from other people who are trying to be good. They hope, by being good, to please God if there is one; or—if they think there is not—at least they hope to deserve approval from good men. But the Christian thinks any good he does comes from the Christ-life inside him. He does not think God will love us because we are good, but that God will make us good because He loves us."

Chapter 8

FAITHFULNESS—A STABILIZING FEATURE OF AN EFFECTIVE RELATIONSHIP

FAITHFULNESS is a quality of being there when you are needed. It entails loyalty, commitment, and caring of the highest degree. It stems from a desire to never let the other person down.

When one is unfaithful in a relationship, trust is destroyed. When trust is destroyed, as we mentioned before, it is most difficult to build it up again.

God is so faithful to us, and He wants us to be faithful to Him and other people, especially those we are closest to. The Scripture tells us that he who is faithful in little things shall be worthy of being entrusted with much.

Did you ever notice that the word "faithful" begins with the word "faith"? A faithful person is a person who is filled with faith, and this faith is what leads him to be faithful in his relationships.

Evelyn Underhill writes, "Faithfulness is the quality of the friend, refusing no test and no trouble, loyal, persevering; not at the mercy of emotional ups and downs or getting tired when things are tiresome.

39

In the interior life of prayer faithfulness points steadily to God and His purposes, away from self and its preoccupations."

Faithfulness is loyalty that stems from love. Those who are strong in love and faith will always be faithful.

Another word for faithfulness is "fidelity," which means "faithful devotion to duty or to one's obligations and vows."

The mindset of a faithful individual is to see others through, not to see through others. It does not matter how many talents you may have; what truly matters is whether you are faithful to the talents, gifts, and calling that God has given to you and to the people He has brought into your life.

Faithfulness helps us to see faith in action. Faith is the evidence of things unseen, but faithfulness is the evidence of what one happens when he exercises faith.

Faithfulness is not a part-time job. It is a full-time job. You can't be just 50% faithful to your spouse. You must be 100% faithful to him or her.

Though it usually is not easy to be faithful and the rewards of faithfulness are additional responsibilities, it is important for us to remain steadfast and immoveable, always abounding in the work of the Lord forasmuch as you know that your labor is never in vain in the Lord. (See 1 Corinthians 15:58.)

There is a cost involved when you choose to be faithful.

Abraham's faith and faithfulness led him to be willing to give up his son. The hundreds of thousands of Christian martyrs throughout the centuries were faithful unto death. They did not count the cost, and we must not either. (If you have not done so, I encourage you to read *Foxe's Book of Martyrs*, a Pure Gold Classic published by Bridge-Logos.)

Max Lucado puts it this way, "I choose faithfulness. . . . Today I will keep my promises. My debtors will not regret their trust. My associates will not question my word. My wife will not question my love. And my children will never fear that their father will not come home."

Faithfulness—a blessed word indeed and a necessary quality in believers. It is as Mother Teresa wrote, "I am not called to be successful; I am called to be faithful."

Chapter 9

GENTLENESS/MEEKNESS— A QUALITY OF STRENGTH IN YOUR RELATIONSHIPS

GENTLENESS and meekness are often seen as being signs of weakness. However, they really are strong qualities that enable the believer to respect others, understand themselves, and become peacemakers in a violent world.

A gentle person never inflicts pain on someone else. A meek person never lords it over another individual. The fact is that gentleness is a very strong force, indeed. It evokes the right kind of toughness—strength of character.

Gentleness and meekness entail humility—a special quality that is hard to find. Nonetheless, these are the qualities that enable us to be led by God's Spirit. They are marks of a true Christian disciple.

When you are walking in meekness, you are walking in peace and joy. When you are gentle with others, you are showing them a way of life that they might not have known before.

Warren Wiersbe defines meekness this way, "Meekness is power under control." I like this quote, because it declares that meekness and gentleness come from power, not from weakness. They come from God who is at work within us.

God is working His purposes out in your life, and one of those purposes is to make you gentle and meek. In order for this to happen though, all pride in your life must be uprooted. God can do this if your will let Him.

God's strength enables us to be meek and gentle, for it is certain that these qualities cannot be created by us. It is an inner beauty that comes from the indwelling presence of the Holy Spirit within us.

What did Jesus mean when He said, "The meek shall inherit the earth" (Matthew 5:5)? I believe He is saying that the meek will be able to enter the Promised Land. It also refers to Psalm 37, which says, "Trust in the Lord and do good; dwell in the land and enjoy safe pasture. . . . A little while and the wicked will be no more; though you look for them, they will not be found. But the meek will inherit the land and enjoy great peace" (Psalm 37:1-2; 10-11).

This is also a prophecy of the time when a new Heaven and a new Earth will be our possession. Yes, the meek will inherit the Earth. I look forward to that great time.

Paul wrote these important words to the Ephesians: ". . . walk worthy of the vocation wherewith ye are called, with all lowliness and meekness, with longsuffering, forbearing one another in love" (Ephesians 4:1-2).

Bring strength into your relationships by walking in gentleness and meekness.

Chapter 10

SELF-CONTROL—LIVING OUT GOD'S COMMANDMENTS IN YOUR RELATIONSHIPS

WHAT do we need to get under control in our lives? There are certain parts of us that may frequently cause problems in our lives, and these definitely call for self-control:

- Our tongues
- Our thoughts
- Our behavior
- Our emotions

We need God's grace to enable us to practice self-control in all areas of our lives. The concept comes from the word "temperance," which means to have mastery over one's thoughts and actions.

Our lusts and passions present us with daily confrontations. We can only avoid these by walking in the Spirit. (See Galatians 5:16.) Frances E. Willard wrote, "Temperance is moderation in the things that are good and total abstinence from the things that are foul."

Self-control requires discipline and it yields contentment in our lives. It involves the denial of selfishness in all its forms.

As we learn to walk in self-control, all these other forms of the self-life wither up and die: self-centeredness, self-righteousness, self-defense, selfishness, self-aggrandizement, self-serving, etc.

Brian Tracy said, "You cannot control what happens to you, but you can control your attitude toward what happens to you, and in that, you will be mastering change rather than allowing it to master you."

Self-control in your relationships is very important. It enables you to listen instead of talking. It enables you to be proactive instead of reactive. It keeps you on an even keel.

Proverbs says, "He that hath no rule over his own spirit is like a city that is broken down, and without walls" (Proverbs 25:28). Such a city is open to all invaders and it has no defense. Practicing self-control helps us to keep our defenses up so that evil thoughts and bad behaviors will not be able to enter our lives.

John Milton wrote, "The command of one's self is the greatest empire a man can aspire unto, and consequently, to be subject to our own passions is the most generous slavery. He who best governs himself is best fitted to govern others. He who reigns within himself and rules his passions, desires and fears is more than a king."

As you can see, self-control is an important component in your relationships with others.

PART II

PRAYERS THAT CHANGE THINGS IN YOUR RELATIONSHIP WITH GOD

Chapter 1

INTIMACY WITH GOD

Draw nigh to God, and he will draw nigh to you.
(James 4:8)

Central Focus: There is a place of quiet rest near to the heart of God. I want to be close to my heavenly Father and to have intimate fellowship with Him. I want to find that place of quiet rest where sin cannot molest.

Prayer: Abba Father, as your child, I want to know you as fully as possible. Help me to be still in your presence and to know you more intimately. As I pray, I am drawing near to you, and I know you are drawing near to me. I want to have true fellowship with you, Father, and with your Son, Jesus Christ. Thank you for your promise that this will bring me fullness of joy.

Because I want to walk in fellowship with you at all times, Father, I will no longer walk in darkness. Instead, I will walk in the light, as you are in the light. This will enhance my fellowship with you and with other believers. Thank you for the blood of Jesus that cleanses me from all sin.

Thank you, Father, for the grace of the Lord Jesus Christ, your amazing love, and the communion of the Holy Ghost. You are my Shepherd, Lord God, and I want to live close to you. Because of your faithfulness in my life, I know I shall never suffer want. I will fear no evil, because I know you are always with me.

The promises of your Word mean so much to me, Father. Truly your Word is a light unto my path and a lamp unto my feet. Help me to walk in the light of your Word always. I know you will never leave me nor forsake me. Thank you, Father.

It thrills me to know that you have reconciled me unto yourself. Help me to continue in the faith, grounded and settled, and not to be moved away from the hope of the gospel. Thank you for the Holy Spirit who bears witness with my spirit that I am a child of God.

Thank you for loving me with an everlasting love, Father. I will always endeavor to be faithful to you. I am so glad to know that you have searched me and known me. You know when I sit down and when I rise up; you discern my thoughts from afar. You search out my path and my lying down and are acquainted with all my ways. Even before a word is on my tongue, behold, O Lord, you know it altogether. Thank you for hemming me in, behind and before, and laying your hand upon me.

You are my God. I seek you earnestly. My soul thirsts for you. My flesh faints for you, as in a dry and weary land where there is no water. I have beheld your power and your glory in the sanctuary. Because your lovingkindness is better than life to me, my lips shall praise you and my soul will be satisfied. With all my heart, soul, and might I will love you for the rest of my days. In Jesus' name I pray, Amen.

Scriptures: Psalm 46:10; James 4:8; 1 John 1:3; 1 John 1:4; 1 John 1:7; 2 Corinthians 13:14; Psalm 23:1; Psalm 23:4; Psalm 119:105; Hebrews 13:5; Colossians 1:21; Colossians 1:23; Romans 8:16; Jeremiah 31:3; Psalm 139:1-24; Psalm 63:1-11; Deuteronomy 6:5.

Personal Affirmation: Knowing that every day with Jesus is sweeter than the day before, I will daily seek God's face, enjoy His grace, and grow in my knowledge of Him. I will seek an intimate relationship with my heavenly Father.

Reflection: *"Too late have I loved You, O Beauty so ancient and so new, too late have I loved You! Behold, You were within me, while I was outside: it was there that I sought You. . . . You were with me, but I was not with You. . . . You have blazed forth with light, and have shone upon me, ... You have sent forth fragrance, and I have drawn in my breath, and I pant after You. You have touched me, and I have burned for Your peace"* (St. Augustine).

Chapter 2

LISTENING TO GOD

My sheep hear my voice, and I know them,
and they follow me.
(John 10:27)

Central Focus: The still, small voice of God's Holy Spirit is speaking to me, and I want my ears to be open to His voice at all times. I want to be able to recognize His voice when He speaks. I will attune my heart to hear Him as He calls to me.

Prayer: Dear Father, my God and my King, thank you for Jesus' promise to His sheep. I want to hear His voice, and I thank you so much that He knows me. Help me to follow Him always. Help me to pay attention to what I hear from your lips. I always want my heart to be open to you. I never want to harden my heart.

I delight myself in you, Lord, and as I do so, you are giving me the desires of my heart. Thank you, Father. I commit my life afresh to you and I trust in you and in so doing I know you will take action in my behalf. Thank you for the promises of your Word, Father.

Open my eyes and my ears, Father, that I will behold your beauty and hear wondrous things from your Word. As I still myself in your presence, listening for your voice, I realize anew how wonderful you are. Lead me in your truth and teach me, for you are the God of my salvation. I wait for you all the day long. Remember your mercy, O Lord, and your steadfast love, for they have been from of old. You are so good and upright, my Father, and I thank you for teaching me so many things. Thank you for leading me into what is right and teaching me your ways.

Speak to me, dear God, while I'm awake and in dreams while I am asleep. Thank you for opening my ears to hear you. Make me to know your ways, O Lord, and teach me your paths. Lead me in your truth and teach me, for you are the God of my salvation, and I wait for you all the day.

Father, I receive your words and I treasure your commandments. Make my ears attentive to wisdom and incline my heart to spiritual understanding. As I call out to you for insight and understanding, I get to know you better. Thank you, Father.

Your Word is fixed firmly in the heavens, dear God, and I thank you for your Word through which you speak to me. Thank you for sending the Holy Spirit to dwell within me. He is my Helper, and I know He is teaching me all things and bringing to my remembrance the things that Jesus has taught. Thank you for the indwelling presence of the Holy Spirit.

Thank you for your love, Lord, and for the truth that you are mighty in the midst of us. It thrills me to know that you are rejoicing over me with joy and you are singing over me with joy. Hallelujah!

I will listen for your voice, Father, because I know you are speaking to me. In Jesus' name, Amen.

Scriptures: John 10:27; Mark 4:24; Hebrews 4:7; Psalm 37:5-6; Psalm 119:18; Psalm 46:10; Psalm 25:5-9; Job 33:14-15; Isaiah 50:4-5; Psalm 25:4-5; Proverbs 2:1-5; Psalm 119:89; John 15:26; Zephaniah 3:17.

Personal Affirmation: Through God's grace I will attune my heart to hear His voice and I will act upon whatever He tells me. As I read His Word, I will listen for His voice. As I pray, I will wait to see what He will say to me.

Reflection: *God's voice is the sweetest voice I've ever heard. He talks with me and He tells me I am His own. There is nothing to compare with the fellowship we share. I just want to soak in His presence.*

Chapter 3

FOLLOWING THE LORD

If ye love me, keep my commandments.
(John 14:15)

Central Focus: We are called to follow God in all things. It is this that will change the world around us.

Prayer: Dear heavenly Father, I want to follow you every step of the way. I love you, and I want to keep your commandments. I believe your promise that shows me the fruits of obedience, and I believe I will be blessed in the city and in the field. I believe you will bless my children and the work I do. I believe your blessings will follow me if I learn to follow you.

Help me to be an imitator of Christ. Thank you for your inspired Word, which is profitable for teaching, reproof, correction, and for training in righteousness. I know that as I learn to follow the teachings of your Word, you will make me into a competent servant who is equipped for every good work. Your Word is a lamp unto my feet and a light unto my path. Help me to walk in the light it sheds every step of my way.

I want to follow you and your ways, Lord. Help me to avoid any way that seems right to man but ends up in death. As for me and my family, we will serve you.

We choose life, not death. With your help, Almighty Father, I will not walk after the flesh, but after the Spirit. I thank you for the truth that the Spirit of life in Christ Jesus has set me free from the law of sin and death.

I know, O Lord, that the way of a man is not in himself. It is not up to me to direct my steps. I will trust in you with all my heart and not lean upon my own understanding. In all my ways I will acknowledge you, and I know you will direct my steps. Thank you, Father.

You have directed my heart into your wonderful love, and I patiently wait for the coming of my Lord Jesus Christ. You have commanded me to keep your precepts diligently, and this I will do, Father, through your grace. I will seek you with my whole heart, and I will avoid iniquity. Then I shall not be ashamed, because I know I have respect for your commandments and your ways.

Blessed are you, O Lord, my rock. Thank you for training my hands for war and my fingers for battle. Help me to walk worthy of the vocation to which you've called me. I will follow you, O God, as your dear child, and I will walk in love, as Christ has loved me.

Teach me how to walk as a child of light and to walk circumspectly, as a wise person, not as a fool. Help me to walk in wisdom toward those who do not believe in you, redeeming the time. I want to walk worthy of you, Father. Thank you for calling me unto your kingdom and glory.

With your help I will walk in grace and truth, in love, in wisdom, and as a child of the light. Thank you for leading me and holding me up.

It is my desire, dear heavenly Father, to always be steadfast, immoveable, and always abounding in your work; for I realize that my labor is never in vain when it is done in your strength and power. In Jesus' name, Amen.

Scriptures: John 14:15; Deuteronomy 28; 1 Corinthians 11:1; 2 Timothy 3:16-17; Psalm 119:105; Proverbs 14:12; Joshua 24:15; Deuteronomy 30:19; Romans 8:1-2; Jeremiah 10:23; Proverbs 3:5-6; 2 Thessalonians 3:5; Psalm 119:2-5; Psalm 144:1; Ephesians 4:1; Ephesians 5:1-2; Ephesians 5:8; Ephesians 5:15; Colossians 4:5; 1 Thessalonians 2:12; 1 Corinthians 15:58.

Personal Affirmation: Jesus said, "Follow me." Where He leads me I will follow. I'll go with Him all the way.

Reflection: *"Almighty God is on our team. He is our faithful Sustainer. When everybody else abandons us, we can count on Him. When nobody else is willing to endure with us, He is there. He is trustworthy, reliable, and consistent. We can depend on Him"* (Charles Stanley).

Chapter 4

WALKING WITH GOD

*If ye walk in my statutes, and keep my
commandments, and do them;
then I will give you rain in due season,
and the land shall yield her increase,
and the trees of the field shall yield their fruit.*

(Leviticus 26:3–4)

Central Focus: To walk with God is to walk in His ways, His truth, His wisdom, His love, and His peace. As I reach up and take hold of His hand, I am determined to walk with Him.

Prayer: O God, my Father, give me your grace, that I would walk in your statutes and keep your commandments. Help me to remember that I walk by faith and not by sight. Your promises are so wonderful to me, and I will walk in all the way that you have commanded me to do. In so doing, I know I shall live and things will go well for me and mine, that I might live long in the land you have given to me.

It encourages me to know that you are not finished with me, Father. I am your workmanship, and I was created in Christ Jesus for good works. Help me to walk in them throughout my life. Father, your Word is a lamp unto my feet and a light unto my path. Help me to walk in the light it sheds each step of my way.

Keep my steps steady according to your promise and do not let iniquity ever have dominion over me. Thank you for the great cloud of witnesses that surrounds me. In light of this, I will lay aside every weight and the sin that does so easily beset me, and I will run the race you have set before me, looking unto Jesus who is the Author and Finisher of my faith.

Like Noah and Enoch, I want to walk with you, Father. Help me to constantly observe all that you have taught me. I thank you that you will be with me to the end of the age. I know you will never leave me nor forsake me. Thank you, Father.

I trust in you, Lord, and I am determined to do good. I will dwell in the land and I will befriend faithfulness. I will delight myself in you, and I know you will give me the desires of my heart. Thank you so much for this prevailing promise from your Word.

Father, it is wonderful to know that you have shown me what is good and what you require of me. It is my desire to always do justice, love kindness, and walk humbly with you. I praise you for your Word, Father, and I will not let it ever depart from my mouth. I will meditate upon it both night and day. I will be careful to do according to all that you have written within it. Thank you for promising to make my way prosperous and to give me good success.

I want to be like the early Christians who walked in the

fear of the Lord and the comfort of the Holy Ghost. Therefore, I draw near to you, Lord, and I know you are drawing near to me. Thank you for your holy presence.

Keep me from ever walking in the counsel of the ungodly, standing in the way of sinners, and sitting in the seat of the scornful. My delight is in your law, Lord God, and in your law I will keep on meditating. The result will be that I shall become like a fruitful tree that is planted by the rivers of water. It is so good to know that you have promised me that my leaf shall not wither and whatever I do shall prosper. Thank you, Father.

I rejoice in your promise that I will abide in your tabernacle and dwell in your holy hill if I walk uprightly, work righteousness, and speak the truth in my heart. Through your grace, loving Father, I will be careful to do these things as I walk with you. In the precious name of Jesus I pray, Amen.

Scriptures: Leviticus 26:3; 2 Corinthians 5:7; Deuteronomy 5:33; Ephesians 2:10; Psalm 119:105; Psalm 119:133; Hebrews 12: 1-2; Genesis 6:9; Genesis 5:22-24; Matthew 28:20; Hebrews 13:5; Psalm 37; Micah 6:8; Joshua 1:8; Acts 9:31; James 4:8; Psalm 1:1-3; Psalm 15:1-2.

Personal Affirmation: Hand in hand and side by side, I choose to walk with God. I have decided to follow Jesus, and I will never turn back.

Reflection: *"True fidelity consists in obeying God in all things, and in following the light that points out our duty, and the grace which guides us; taking as our* *rule of life the intention to please God in all things, and to do always not only what is acceptable to Him. . . . To this sincere desire to do the will of God, we must add a cheerful spirit, that is not overcome when it has failed, but begins again and again to do better. . . ."* (Francois Fenelon).

Chapter 5

SEEKING GOD

But if from thence thou shalt seek the Lord thy
God, thou shalt find him, if thou seek him with all
thy heart and with all thy soul.

(Deuteronomy 4:29)

Central Focus: Seeking God leads us into His presence where there is fullness of joy and there are pleasures forevermore. (See Psalm 16:11.)

Prayer: Lord God, I seek you with all my heart and soul. Thank you for your promise which tells me that those who seek you diligently will find you. Help me to seek you diligently, Father. I believe your Word, which tells me that I will find you when I seek you with all my heart, and I believe that you will restore my fortunes as I do so. Thank you, Father.

With my whole heart I seek you, Lord. Don't let me wander from your commandments. As I seek you, I commit my cause and my life to you, because I know you do innumerable great and mighty things. O God, you are my God; earnestly I seek you; my soul thirsts for you; my flesh faints for you, as in a dry and thirsty land where there is no water.

Thank you for your promise that I will not lack any

good thing because I am seeking you. Father, through your grace I will seek first your kingdom and your righteousness, and I know that, as I do so, you will add everything unto me. Praise your holy name.

I love seeking your face. I will seek you, your strength, and your presence continually. Help me to keep your testimonies. Increase my faith, Lord, because I know it is impossible to please you without faith. As I draw near to you and seek you, I know that you are rewarding me.

Father, I realize that you have set before me life and good, death and evil. I choose to obey you by loving you, walking in your ways, and keeping your commandments. Thank you for your promise to bless me and mine.

It is a wonderful adventure for me to be led by your Spirit, Lord. I am fully persuaded that nothing shall ever separate me from your love in Christ Jesus, my Lord. As I ask, I know you will answer me. As I seek, I know I will find. As I knock, I know it will be opened unto me. Thank you, Father.

Throughout my life I will seek you, Lord, while you may be found. I will call upon you when you are near. I will forsake all wickedness and wrong thoughts, as I return to you. Your compassion for me is overwhelming and I thank you for abundantly pardoning me. In the name of my Lord Jesus Christ I pray, Amen.

Scriptures: Deuteronomy 4:29; Proverbs 8:17; Jeremiah 29:12-14; Psalm 119:10; Job 5:8-9; Psalm 63:1; Psalm

34:10; Matthew 6:33; 1 Chronicles 16:11; Psalm 119:2; Hebrews 11:6; Deuteronomy 30:15-16; Romans 8:14; Romans 8:38-39; Matthew 7:7-8; Isaiah 55:6-7.

Personal Affirmation: I will seek the Lord afresh every day of my life.

Reflection: *"I suddenly saw that all the time it was not I who had been seeking God, but God who had been seeking me. I had made myself the center of my own existence and had my back turned to God"* (Bede Griffiths).

Chapter 6

WORSHIPING THE LORD

But the hour cometh, and now is, when the true worshippers shall worship the Father in spirit and in truth: for the Father seeketh such to worship him.

(John 4:23).

Central Focus: Learning how to worship the Father in spirit and in truth is one of my primary goals in life. Worshiping the Lord is so refreshing to me.

Prayer: Heavenly Father, I want to be one of those worshipers you are seeking, a worshiper who worships you in spirit and in truth. Teach me how to be such a worshiper.

Through Christ I will continually offer up to you a sacrifice of praise. The fruit of my lips will ever give praise to you. I will bless you at all times, Father. Your praise shall continually be in my mouth. My soul shall make its boast in you, Lord, and the humble will hear it and rejoice. I magnify you, Lord, and I exalt your name.

I will shout joyfully to you, Lord, as I enter your gates with thanksgiving and go into your courts with praise. I will give thanks to you and bless your name. You are holy, O Lord, and you are enthroned on the praises of your people.

I want your praises to be in my mouth, and I will carry a two-edged sword in my hand, which is your powerful Word. Your name alone is to be exalted. I will rejoice in you always. Thank you for leading me into worship, Lord, and for showing me that I must serve only you.

I would like to be like Paul and Silas who sang hymns and praised you while they were in prison. The result of their worship was that a miracle occurred and they were released from prison. Thank you for that miracle, Father.

I give thanks to you for who you are and for all you've done for me. Thank you for your loving-kindness, which is everlasting. I will ever sing to you with thanksgiving and sing praises to you.

Help me to show others the importance of praise and worship, so that everything that has breath will learn to praise you, Father. Praise the Lord! It is good to sing praises to you, Father. Indeed, it is most pleasant and wonderful.

In everything I will give thanks, for I know this is your will in Christ Jesus concerning me. Thank you, Father.

It is a very good thing to give thanks to you, Father, and to sing praises to your name, O Most High. Help me to show forth your loving-kindness every morning and your faithfulness every night. You have made me glad, Father, through your work. I will triumph in the work of your hands.

How great are your works, O Lord, and your thoughts

are very deep. It is through worship that I get to know you and understand your mysteries. Thank you for worship, Father.

In Jesus' name I pray, Amen.

Scriptures: John 4:23; Hebrews 13:15; Psalm 34:1-3; Psalm 100:1-4; Psalm 22:3; Psalm 149:6; Psalm 147:13; Philippians 4:4; Luke 4:8; Acts 16:25-26; 2 Chronicles 20:21-22; Psalm 147:7; Psalm 150:6; Psalm 147:1; 1 Thessalonians 5:16-18; Psalm 92.

Personal Affirmation: I meet God through worship, and I get to know Him more fully. I will worship Him in spirit and in truth.

Reflection: *"It is in the process of being worshiped that God communicates His presence to men"* (C.S. Lewis).

PART III

FRUITFUL PRAYERS THAT
CHANGE THINGS IN ALL
YOUR RELATIONSHIPS—
THESE PRAYERS ARE
BASED ON THE FRUIT
OF THE SPIRIT.
(SEE GALATIANS 5:22-23.)

Chapter 1

LOVE

God is love.

(1 John 4:8)

Central Focus: We must love God, others, and ourselves. Such love has the power to change all our relationships, and it has the power to change the world as well.

Prayer: Loving Father, I know you are love, and I want to walk in your love every step of the way in all the relationships in my life. I walk away from all bitterness, wrath, anger, clamor, and evil speaking. Help me to be kind and tenderhearted toward others and to forgive those who have wronged me in any way, even as you have forgiven me for Christ's sake. I want to be your follower, Father, as your dear child.

Thank you for loving the world so much that you gave your only begotten Son, that whosoever believes in Him would not perish, but have eternal life. Help me to love others in the same way, Father, that I would give sacrificially to those in need.

In everything I am more than a conqueror through Jesus Christ, my Lord, and I am certain that neither death nor life, angels, rulers, present things, and future things shall not be able to separate me from your marvelous love. Thank you for this Bible promise, Father.

Help me to owe no one anything except to love them. Help me to serve others through love. Help me to bear with others through love. I want to love others earnestly from a pure heart. Help me to love others, because I know that love comes from you and the love you give to me assures me that I know you and have been born of you. Thank you, Lord.

Help me to love my enemies and to pray for them. Help me to be perfect in love as you are perfect, Father. It is my heart's desire to abide in the love of Jesus, that His joy would live within me. I realize, Lord, that in order for me to do so, I must keep your commandments. Thank you for calling me your friend. Thank you for choosing and appointing me, that I would bear abiding fruit for you.

Your prayer promise is that you will give me whatever I ask you for, so I now ask, dear God, that you will so fill my heart with love that I will love others at all times. Help me to bear the fruit of love in all the relationships and responsibilities of my life. In Jesus' name, Amen.

Scriptures: 1 John 4:8; Ephesians 5:2; Ephesians 4:31; Ephesians 5:1; John 3:16; Romans 8:37–38; Romans 13:8; Galatians 5:13; Ephesians 4:2; 1 Peter 1:22; Matthew 5:43–48; John 15:9–17.

Personal Affirmation: I will love God with all my heart, soul, mind, and strength, and I will love my neighbor as myself. I want to be a vessel of love in my Father's hands.

Reflection: *"God loves you just the way you are, but He refuses to leave you that way. He wants you to be just like Jesus"* (Max Lucado).

Chapter 2

JOY

The joy of the Lord is my strength.
(Nehemiah 8:10)

Central Focus: Joy is like a sweet-water well that bubbles up from deep within and overflows to others. This is the joy that Jesus gives.

Prayer: Father, I ask for your joy to be my experience, for I know that your joy is my strength. Because you always defend me, I rejoice as I put my complete trust in you. I will ever be joyful in you, Father. Thank you for showing me the pathway of life. In your presence is fullness of joy; at your right hand there are pleasures forevermore.

Your joy within me causes me to bless you at all times. Your praise shall be continually in my mouth. My soul will make its boast in you, and the humble will hear and be glad. Thank you, Father. I will praise you, O Lord my God, with all my heart, and I will glorify your name forevermore.

You are my salvation, O God. I will trust in you and not be afraid. You are my strength and my song. Therefore, with joy I will draw waters from your wells of salvation. Thank you for giving me beauty for ashes, the oil of joy for mourning, and the garment of praise for the spirit of heaviness. I now know that I shall be a tree of righteousness, your planting, Lord, and I know you will be glorified through me.

Your Word, dear Father, is the joy and rejoicing of my heart, for I am called by your name, O Lord God of hosts. I will rejoice in you, O Lord, and I will joy in you, the God of my salvation. Help me to learn to rejoice in you at all times.

Lord, I ask that your joy would remain within me, because I know this will make my joy full. Thank you so much for joy. You have shown me, Father, that your Kingdom does not consist of meat and drink, but of righteousness, peace, and joy in the Holy Spirit. Hallelujah!

Fill me afresh with your Spirit, Lord God, that I might make melody in my heart unto you. It is so true, as your Word declares, that a merry heart does one well, like a medicine. Even when I fall into diverse temptations, Lord, I will count it all joy.

I will be glad and rejoice in you, and I will give honor to you. Let me bear the fruit of joy in all the relationships and responsibilities of my life. Thank you for joy, dear Father.

Scriptures: Nehemiah 8:10; Psalm 5:11; Psalm 16:11; Psalm 34:1-2; Psalm 86:12; Isaiah 12:1-2; Isaiah 61:3; Jeremiah 15:16; Habakkuk 3:17-18; Matthew 5:11-12; John 15:11; Romans 14:17; Ephesians 5:18-19; Proverbs 17:22; James

1:12; Revelation 19:7.

Personal Affirmation: I will be a joyful person no matter what the outward circumstances might be.

Reflection: *"The Christian owes it to the world to be supernaturally joyful"* (A.W. Tozer).

Chapter 3

PEACE

*The peace of God, which passeth all
understanding, shall keep your hearts and minds
through Christ Jesus.*
(Philippians 4:7)

Central Focus: God's supernatural peace is able to
guard my heart and mind and keep me free from all
anxiety and fear.

Prayer: Abba Father, I will rejoice in you always because
of the wonderful peace you've given to me. I will not be
worried or anxious about anything, but in everything
by prayer and supplication with thanksgiving I will let
my requests be made unto you. As a result, I know
that your peace which passes all understanding will
keep my heart and my mind through Christ Jesus.
Thank you, Father.

Jesus gave His peace to me, not as the world gives.
Therefore, I will not let my heart be troubled or afraid.
Thank you, Father, for justifying me through faith. This
gives me great peace with you through the Lord Jesus
Christ. Thank you for your promise that you, the Lord of
peace, will give me peace at all times and in every way.

Help me to keep my mind stayed on you and to trust

you, for I know this will bring about great peace in my life. Help me always, Father, to turn from evil and do good. Help me to seek and pursue your peace. Through your grace, I will let your peace rule in my heart and I will be thankful.

Help me to live in peace with everyone. I love your law, O Lord, and I know nothing will cause me to stumble because I know your Word. I will lie down and sleep in peace, for you alone, O Lord, make me dwell in safety. Thank you, Father.

Help me to make all my ways be pleasing to you, Lord, because I know that this is the key to peace with my enemies. Impart your righteousness to me, Father, for I know your righteousness in my life will lead to peace, quietness, and confidence.

Thank you for Jesus who has overcome the world. Because of Him, I know I will enjoy peace for the rest of my days. Thank you for giving me your strength and blessing me with peace. Thank you, God of hope, for filling me with all joy and peace as I trust in you. This causes me to overflow with hope through the power of the Holy Spirit.

Help me to bear the fruit of peace in all the relationships and responsibilities of my life. In Jesus' name I pray, Amen.

Scriptures: Philippians 4:4-7; John 14:27; Romans 5:1; 2 Thessalonians 3:16; Isaiah 26:3; Psalm 34:13; Colossians 3:15; Romans 12:18; Proverbs 16:7; Psalm 4:8; John 16:33;

Psalm 29:11; Romans 15:13.

Personal Affirmation: I am determined to walk in peace through the power of the Holy Spirit.

Reflection: *"My depths are held by peace. The surface may be disturbed; it's the depths that count"* (E. Stanley Jones).

CHAPTER 4

PATIENCE

Rejoicing in hope; patient in tribulation;
continuing instant in prayer.
(Romans 12:12)

Central Focus: I want patience to have its perfect work in my life. (See James 1:4.)

Prayer: Father, through your grace I will rejoice in hope, be patient in tribulation, and continue instant in prayer. I will be still before you and wait patiently for you. Help me to be quick to hear, slow to speak, and slow to anger.

I want to be patient, Father, until the coming of the Lord, in the same way that a farmer waits for the precious fruit of the earth with patience. Help me to endure hardship and evil with patience, as you strengthen me with your glorious might for all endurance and patience with joy.

Help me to remember this truth from your Word: "Better is the end of a thing than its beginning, and the patient in spirit is better than the proud in spirit." I want to be patient in spirit, Lord. Thank you for giving me patience and endurance, Lord, for through them I will receive what you've promised to me. Thank you, Father.

As I wait upon you, I know my strength is being renewed and I am mounting up with wings like an eagle. This will enable me to run and not be weary and to walk and not faint. Thank you for your power, Lord. Help me to hear your Word and hold it fast in an honest and good heart so that I will be able to bear fruit with patience. I never want to be sluggish. Instead, with your help I will be an imitator of those who through faith and patience inherited the promises.

I will put on, then, as your chosen one, a compassionate heart, kindness, humility, meekness, and patience so as to walk in a manner worthy of you, my Father, fully pleasing to you, and bearing fruit in every good work as I increase in my knowledge of you.

Help me to walk in a manner that is worthy of the calling to which I've been called, with all humility and gentleness, with patience, and bearing with others in love. Help me always to be patient with other people. As I wait patiently for you, Lord, I know you are inclining to me and hearing my cry. Thank you, Father.

Help me to bear the fruit of patience in all the relationships and responsibilities of my life. In the name of Jesus I pray, Amen.

Scriptures: Romans 12:12; Psalm 37:7; James 1:19; James 5:7; 2 Timothy 2:24; Colossians 1:11; Ecclesiastes 7:8; Hebrews 10:36; Isaiah 40:31; Luke 8:15; Hebrews 6:12; Colossians 3:12; Colossians 1:10; Ephesians 4:1-2; 1 Thessalonians 5:14.

Personal Affirmation: I choose to be a patient person for the rest of my life.

Reflection: *God's timing is perfect. "Patience is not passive; on the contrary it is active; it is concentrated strength. There is one form of hope which is never unwise, and which certainly does not diminish with the increase of knowledge. In that form it changes its name, and we call it patience"* (Bulwer-Lytton).

Chapter 5

KINDNESS

And be ye kind one to another, tenderhearted,
forgiving one another.
(Ephesians 4:32)

Central Focus: Random acts of kindness change people's lives. I want to be kind to others and to be creative in applying kindness to all of the relationships in my life.

Prayer: O God, my Father, thank you for the fruit of the Spirit in my life. Kindness is one fruit of the Spirit, and I want to walk in kindness toward others always. Help me to be kind, tenderhearted, and loving in all my relationships.

How precious is your loving-kindness, O God. I take refuge in the shadow of your wings. Your loving-kindness is great toward me, and your truth is everlasting. Thank you, Father. Help me to be a kind and generous person, one who follows your Word, which says that a generous person will prosper and he who waters will himself be watered.

Your Word declares, "What is desirable in a person is kindness." Fulfill your desire in me, Lord, throughout this day by giving me the grace to be kind in all my dealings with others.

In obedience to you, Lord, I will love my enemies, do good to those who hate me, bless those who curse me, and pray for those who mistreat me. I will do to others as I would have them do to me. Help me to be merciful as you are merciful, Father. Keep me from judging others, that I would not be judged by others. I never want to be condemning or condescending toward others.

It is my desire to give to others. Thank you for this promise, Lord: "Good measure, pressed down, shaken together, running over, they will pour into your lap. For by your standard of measure it will be measured to you in return."

I believe your Word, which says, "It is more blessed to give than to receive." Father, I know that kindness comes from love—your love—and it is a fruit of the Holy Spirit in my life. Help me to bear the fruit of kindness in all the relationships and responsibilities of my life. Help me not to lose heart in doing good.

With your help, I will do good as to you, Lord, and not just to my fellow-men, and I will do nothing from selfishness or empty conceit, but with humility of mind I will regard others as being more important than myself. I will not only look out for my own personal interests, but for the interests of others as well. Help me to have the attitude of Christ, who, although He existed in the form of God, did not regard equality with God a thing to be grasped, but emptied himself, taking the form of a bond servant, and being made in the likeness of men.

Thank you for your love, Father, which enables me to love others. Let the love of the brethren continue in my life always, and help me not to neglect to show hospitality to strangers. I realize, Lord, that some have entertained angels without realizing it by showing such hospitality. I would like to do so as well.

Help me to walk in your wisdom, Father. Your wisdom is pure, peaceable, reasonable, full of mercy and good fruits, unwavering, and without hypocrisy. Help me to sow the seed whose fruit is righteousness and to sow it in peace, as I endeavor to make peace through kindness. In Jesus' name I pray, Amen.

Scriptures: Ephesians 4:32; Psalm 36:7; Psalm 117:2; Proverbs 11:25; Luke 6:27–31; Luke 6:36–38; Acts 20:35; 1 Corinthians 13; Galatians 6:9; Ephesians 6:7; Philippians 2:3-7; Philippians 4:4–8; 1 John 3:19; Hebrews 13:1-2.

Personal Affirmation: God's kindness and the kindness of others in my life have always meant so much to me. This propels me to be kind toward others, and I commit myself to be kind in all the relationships of my life.

Reflection: *"Life is made up, not of great sacrifices or duties, but of little things, in which smiles and kindnesses, and small obligations, given habitually, are what win and preserve the heart and secure comfort"* (Sir H. Davy).

Chapter 6

GOODNESS

Let love be without dissimulation. Abhor that which is evil; cleave to that which is good.

(Romans 12:9)

Central Focus: All goodness comes from God, and He lives within me. I will let His goodness come forth from me in all the relationships of my life.

Prayer: Almighty God, help me to love others without hypocrisy and to cleave to that which is good. How abundant is your goodness, which you have stored up for those who fear you and work for those who take refuge in you. I take refuge in you now, Father.

Thank you for your wisdom. Help me to walk in your wisdom, as I endeavor to keep my conduct good in my relationships with others. You have shown me what I need to do, Father, to walk in goodness. You have shown me what you require of me, that I should do justice, love kindness, and walk humbly with you. Through your grace, I will do so.

Thank you for your inspired Word, which is profitable in my life for teaching, reproof, correction, and for training in righteousness. Your Word is a lamp unto my feet and a light unto my path. Help me to walk in the light it sheds each step of my way.

Thank you, Father, for your divine power, which has given me all things that pertain to life and godliness through the knowledge of Him who has called us to glory, virtue, and goodness. Thank you for your exceedingly great and precious promises through which I am able to partake of your divine nature, having escaped the corruption that is in the world through lust.

Giving all diligence, therefore, I will add virtue and goodness to my faith. I will add knowledge to my virtue and goodness. I will add temperance to my knowledge and patience to my godliness. I will add brotherly kindness to godliness and charity to brotherly kindness.

As I do these things, I know I shall be fruitful in the knowledge of my Lord Jesus Christ. In light of this, I will always avoid evil and do good. I will seek peace. Help me, Father, to be compassionate, to love others, and to be courteous and kind. Help me to refrain my tongue from evil and to never speak guileful words.

Give me the grace I need to bear the fruit of goodness in all the relationships and responsibilities of my life. In Jesus' precious name, Amen.

Scriptures: Romans 12:9; Psalm 31:19; James 3:13; Micah 6:8; 2 Timothy 3:16; Psalm 119:105; 2 Peter 1:4-8; 1 Peter 3:1-11.

Personal Affirmation: Realizing that all goodness comes from God and not from myself, I will let His goodness come forth in all my relationships.

Reflection: *"But the Christian thinks any good he does comes from the Christ-life inside him. He does not think God will love us because we are good, but that God will make us good because He loves us"* (C.S. Lewis).

Chapter 7

FAITHFULNESS

Thus shall ye do in the fear of the Lord, faithfully, and with a perfect heart.

(2 Chronicles 19:9)

Central Focus: The goal is faithfulness in all my relationships. I want others to trust me without any reservations whatsoever.

Prayer: Whatever I do, Lord God, I want to do faithfully and with a perfect heart. Help me accomplish this important goal through your grace and power. I respect you, honor you, and adore you, Father, and I want always to serve you faithfully with all my heart. As I consider what great things you have done for me, I am truly overwhelmed and grateful.

Help me never to let steadfast love and faithfulness forsake me. I will bind them around my neck and write them on the tablet of my heart. I want to walk in love and faithfulness throughout my life. Help me, Father.

Great is your faithfulness, O God, my Father. I want to be faithful like you, for your faithfulness reaches to the skies. I thank Christ Jesus my Lord, who has strengthened me and has considered me faithful, putting me into His service.

Lord, I want to be like the saints of Ephesus who were faithful in Christ Jesus. I also want to be like Timothy who was Paul's faithful son in the Lord. Help me to always be your good and faithful servant. I realize that faithfulness in little things will enable me to be put in charge of many things and enable me to enter into my Master's joy. Thank you, Father.

With your help I will be faithful in all my vows, and I will not allow my speech to cause me to sin. Whatever I do I will do heartily as unto you, Lord, and not unto men, knowing that from you I will receive the reward of the inheritance. I will always serve the Lord Christ.

Help me to be faithful with finances and in the use of things that belong to others. I want to be known as a faithful person. Realizing that being faithful means being full of faith, I will grow in faith and in the nurture and admonition of the Lord. Help me to share your Word faithfully, for this is the source of faith in my life. Be merciful to me, Father, that I might be faithful always.

Thank you so much for the fruit of faithfulness, which I want to bear in all the relationships and responsibilities of my life.

Scriptures: 2 Chronicles 19:9; 1 Samuel 12:24; Proverbs 3:3; Lamentations 3:23; Psalm 36:5; 1 Timothy 1:2; Ephesians 1:1; 1 Corinthians 4:7; Matthew 25:21; Ecclesiastes 5:4–6; Colossians 3:23–24; Luke 16:11–13; Ephesians 6:4; Jeremiah 23:28; 1 Corinthians 7:25.

Personal Affirmation: Faithfulness builds trust in every relationship. I want to be a person who is faithful and full of faith at all times.

Reflection: *"The faithful person is dependable. We can put our full faith in him. Faithfulness is love performing its prowess, never growing weary"* (John M. Drescher).

Chapter 8

GENTLENESS/MEEKNESS

To speak evil of no man, to be no brawlers, [but]
gentle, shewing meekness unto all men.

(Titus 3:2)

Central Focus: Gentleness is a fruit of the Spirit.
Meekness is not weakness; it is strength clothed with
a sweet spirit.

Prayer: Father-God, I want to be gentle in all my
dealings with others. I want to show meekness to
others at all times. As I sanctify you in my heart, I will
be ready to always give to people who ask me a reason
for the hope that I have within me in all gentleness
and meekness.

I want to be like you, Father, and I know your gentleness
has made me great. Help me not to strive but to be
gentle unto all, apt to teach, and patient. Help me
to walk in your wisdom, which is pure, peaceable,
gentle, and easy to be entreated. Your wisdom is full
of mercy and good fruits. It is without partiality and
without hypocrisy.

Lord, if I see someone who is overtaken in a fault,
help me to restore him/her in the spirit of meekness,
considering myself, lest I also be tempted. I will take

your yoke upon me, Lord, and learn of you, for I know you are meek and lowly in heart. In this way I will find rest for my soul.

As I pray, I am putting on, as one of your elect, bowels of mercies, kindness, humility, patience, and meekness. Help me to be like Paul who was gentle in the same way that a nurse cherishes the children she cares for.

I choose to lay aside all filthiness and naughtiness as I receive your engrafted Word with meekness. Help me to walk in your Word every day, Father. I will follow after righteousness, godliness, faith, love, patience, and meekness. Thank you, Lord.

Thank you for your wonderful promise to the meek, that we shall inherit the Earth. I will let my moderation be known to all by the way I love, for I know that the Lord is at hand. Help me always to seek meekness and gentleness, Father, and to seek you with all my heart.

Let me bear the fruit of gentleness and meekness in all the relationships of my life. In Jesus' name, Amen.

Scriptures: Titus 3:2; 1 Peter 3:5; Psalm 18:35; 2 Timothy 2:24-26; James 3:17; Galatians 6:1; Matthew 11:29; Colossians 3:12; 1 Thessalonians 2:7; James 1:21; 1 Timothy 6:11; Matthew 5:5; Zephaniah 3:3.

Personal Affirmation: I desire to be a meek and gentle person. I know that God will give me this desire of my heart.

Reflection: *"The word* gentle *was rarely heard before* *the Christian era, and the word* gentleman *was not known. This high quality of character was a direct by-product of Christian faith"* (Billy Graham).

Chapter 9

SELF-CONTROL

Like a city whose walls are broken down
is a man who lacks self-control.
(Proverbs 25:28, NIV)

Central Focus: Self-control (temperance) is a fruit of the Spirit. It is one of the most important ways in which we can love ourselves. God wants us to be self-controlled.

Prayer: Heavenly Father, I do not want to be like a city with broken-down walls. Instead, I want to exercise self-control at all times. Help me, Father, to be a patient person and someone who controls his temper.

Through this prayer and my daily devotions I will prepare my mind for action. I will be self-controlled, and I will set my hope fully on the grace that will be given when Jesus Christ is revealed. I choose to not be like others who are asleep. Instead, I will be alert and self-controlled. Thank you for giving me the grace to do these things, Father.

Since I belong to the day, I will be self-controlled, putting on faith and love as a breastplate and the hope of salvation as a helmet. Help me to keep my head in all situations, to endure hardship, to do the work of an evangelist, and to discharge my duties according to your will.

Help me, Father, to practice self-control in all areas, including eating and drinking. In order to be self-controlled, I seek your help to put to death anything that comes from the earthly nature, including lust, impurity, evil desires, and greed. Because of these things, your wrath will fall upon mankind.

Through your grace I will rid myself of anger, rage, malice, slander, and filthy language. Father, I want to learn how to control my body in a way that is holy and honorable. It is my choice, dear Lord, to be quick to listen, slow to speak, and slow to anger, because I realize that anger never accomplishes your will.

Help me to bridle my tongue, Father. I cry unto you. Make haste unto me. Give ear unto my voice as I cry out to you. Let my prayer be set forth before you as incense and the lifting up of my hands as the evening sacrifice. Set a watch, O Lord, before my mouth; keep the door of my lips. Incline not my heart to any wicked thing.

Because of your mercies to me, I present my body as a living sacrifice, holy and acceptable unto you, because I know this is my reasonable service to you. Through your grace, Father, I will not be conformed to this world. Instead, I will be transformed by the renewing of my mind, that I might prove what your good, acceptable, and perfect will is. Thank you, Father.

In the mighty name of Jesus, I pray. Amen.

Scriptures: Proverbs 15:28; Proverbs 16:32; 1 Peter 1:13; 1 Thessalonians 5:8; 2 Timothy 4:5; Proverbs 23:20–21; Colossians 3:5–8; 1 Thessalonians 4:4; James 1:19–20; James 1:26; Psalm 14:1–4; Romans 12:1–2.

Personal Affirmation: The Holy Spirit lives within me. Leaning on His indwelling presence, I will practice self-control every day of my life.

Reflection: *"I choose self-control. I will be drunk only by joy. I will be impassioned only by faith. I will be influenced only by God. I will be taught only by Christ. I choose self-control"* (Max Lucado).

PART IV

PRAYERS THAT CHANGE THINGS IN YOUR FAMILY RELATIONSHIPS

Chapter 1

YOUR RELATIONSHIP WITH YOUR WIFE

Submitting yourself to one another in the fear of God.
(Ephesians 5:21)

Central Focus: As a husband, I want to learn to love my wife as Christ loved His Church and gave himself for it. (See Ephesians 5:25.)

Prayers: Dear heavenly Father, thank you for the wife you've given to me. She opens her mouth with wisdom and the law of kindness is on her tongue. Help me to listen to her wisdom at all times, dear Father. She works hard, and always takes care of me and our family.

I love her so much, and I want to be creative in learning how to show my love to her. I will not forget to render to my wife the benevolence which is her due. I will never defraud her, Father, in any way. I thank you, Father, for her in the name of the Lord Jesus Christ. Help us to submit ourselves to each other in the fear of you.

Through your grace, Father, I will learn to love my wife as Christ loves His Church and gave himself for it. I want to give myself up for my wife, Lord. I want to love her more than I love myself and my own body. I left my parents in order to be joined to my wife, and now we have become one.

Help me to dwell with my wife according to spiritual knowledge and to give honor to her at all times. Thank you, Father, for making us heirs together of the grace of life, that our prayers would not be hindered.

Bless the fountain of my life, Father, as I rejoice in the wife of my youth. She truly is a loving doe and a graceful deer. I am totally captivated by her love. Thank you, Father. I want to show her my love every day of my life.

Father, I am very grateful for my wife's noble character. She is the crown of my life. I thank you for leading me to this good woman and I thank you for the favor you've given to me. My wife is prudent and she came to me from you, Father. Help me to remember to be faithful to her at all times, Lord. With your help I will lead a blameless life.

Thank you, Father, for the nobility that my wife demonstrates. She is worth far more than rubies to me. Help me to bring happiness to her.

Thank you for your great love, Father. I want to model your love in my relationship with my wife. Because you dwell in me, I know your love will come forth in my marital relationship. Though I know that many women do virtuously, I truly believe that my wife excels them all. Bless her, Father.

In Jesus' name I pray, Amen.

Scriptures: Proverbs 31:26-27; 1 Corinthians 7:3-5; Ephesians 5:20-21; Ephesians 5:25-33; 1 Peter 3:7; Proverbs 5:18-19; Proverbs 12:4; Proverbs 18:22; Proverbs 19:14; Proverbs 20:6-7; Proverbs 31:10; Deuteronomy 24:5; 1 John 4:11-18; Proverbs 31:29.

Personal Affirmation: I love my wife! I will ever do my best to show my love to her and to serve her with all my heart.

Reflection: *"A happy man marries the girl he loves; a happier man loves the girl he marries"* (Anonymous).

Chapter 2

YOUR RELATIONSHIP WITH YOUR HUSBAND

If any [husbands] *obey not the word,*
they also may without the word be won by the
conversation of their wives.

(1 Peter 3:1-2)

Central Focus: As a wife, I want to learn to love, serve, and respect my husband at all times.

Prayer: Heavenly Father, help me always to be sober, to love my husband, to love my children, to be discreet, chaste, and a good home keeper, that your Word will not be blasphemed. Help me to be in subjection to my husband, that he would behold my chaste conversation and be drawn more toward you.

I want to render due benevolence to my husband, and never to defraud him in any way. Giving thanks always to you, Father, in the name of my Lord Jesus Christ, I desire to serve my husband as I submit myself unto you. Thank you for his willingness to serve me. I reverence and respect my husband, Father.

Help me to be a prudent wife, Father. Help me to ever captivate my husband with my love. I never want to be a quarrelsome or complaining wife. Help me to build my family and my home according to your ways.

I want to reverence and respect the husband you've given to me, Lord, and I want to honor him always. Help me to notice him, regard him, honor him, prefer him, venerate, and esteem him. It is my desire, Lord God, to defer to my husband, praise him, love him, and admire him exceedingly.

Help me to conduct myself in a manner that is pure and modest, as I reverence my husband. To reverence him means to honor, esteem, appreciate, prize, adore, admire, be devoted to, deeply love, and enjoy my husband. Thank you, Lord, for making this possible for me to do.

Through your grace I will maintain the unfading beauty of a gentle and quiet spirit, which is of great worth to you, Father. I want my husband's heart to safely trust me. I will do him good and not evil throughout my life.

Help me to gird my loins with strength and to strengthen my arms. May strength and honor be my clothing. I will rejoice in you, Lord, and I know that your joy is my strength. Teach me how to open my mouth with wisdom, Lord, and to let my tongue speak forth the law of kindness.

Help me to maintain our household well and to never be lazy about the responsibilities you've given to me.

Thank you for my husband, Father. Bless him in every way.

In Jesus' name I pray, Amen.

Scriptures: Titus 2:4-5; 1 Peter 3:1-2; 1 Corinthians 7:3-5; Ephesians 5:20-24; Proverbs 19:14; Proverbs 5:19; Proverbs 19:13; Proverbs 21:19; Proverbs 14:1; Ephesians 5:33; 1 Peter 3:2; 1 Peter 3:3-4; Proverbs 31:11-12; Proverbs 31:17; Nehemiah 8:10; Proverbs 31:26; Proverbs 31:27.

Personal Affirmation: I have the best husband in the world. My desire is to love, honor, and serve him for the rest of my life.

Reflection: *"A successful marriage requires falling in love many times, and always with the same person"* (Mignon McLaughlin).

Chapter 3

YOUR RELATIONSHIP WITH YOUR CHILDREN

Train up a child in the way he should go: and when he is old, he will not depart from it.
(Proverbs 22:6)

Central Focus: Being a parent is an awesome privilege. My children are very precious to me. My heart's desire is to bring them up in the nurture and admonition of the Lord. (See Ephesians 6:4.)

Prayer: Abba Father, you have shown me what it means to be an effective parent, and I want to model my parenting after yours. Help me to train up my children in the way that they should go, so that when they are older, they will not depart from your ways. Thank you for choosing me and my family. As for me and my house, we will serve you. Help us to keep your way, O Lord, by doing righteousness and justice at all times.

I want my children to be taught by you, Father, that they would experience your peace throughout their lives. Keep me from ever discouraging my children by provoking them in any way. Help me to remember my responsibility for teaching your Word to my children. I will teach your ways to my children, and we shall talk of your Word within our house.

I want my children to know how faithful you are, Father. Help me to remember the Golden Rule in my relationship with my children—to treat them as I like to be treated. I pray, Lord God, that my faith will be passed on to my children in the same way that Timothy had the faith of his grandmother Lois and his mother, Eunice.

May I learn how to discipline my children wisely, for your Word says that if I love my children, I will discipline them. The result of such discipline will give me rest and it will delight my heart. Thank you, Father. In my discipline of my children I never want to anger them. Instead, I want to bring them up in your discipline and instruction, Lord.

My children are a blessing and an inheritance from you, Father. Thank you for them. They are good and perfect gifts to me that come directly from you. I will cherish my relationship with them always.

In Jesus' name I pray, Amen.

Scriptures: Proverbs 22:6; Joshua 24:15; Genesis 18:19; Isaiah 54:13; Colossians 3:21; Deuteronomy 4:9; Deuteronomy 6:6-9; Isaiah 38:19; Matthew 7:12; 2 Timothy 1:5; Proverbs 13:24; Proverbs 29:17; Ephesians 6:4; Psalm 127:3-5; James 1:17.

Personal Affirmation: I will become an effective parent as I apply the principles of God's Word to my relationship with my children.

Reflection: *"The bond that links your true family is not* *one of blood, but of respect and joy in each other's life"* (Richard David Bach).

Chapter 4

YOUR RELATIONSHIP WITH YOUR PARENTS

Honour thy father and thy mother: that thy days may be long upon the land which the Lord thy God giveth thee.

(Exodus 20:12)

Central Focus: My parents deserve my honor and my respect, because I've learned so much from them. I want my relationship with them to be loving and strong.

Prayer: Dear God, my loving Father, help me to relate to my parents in the right way. Throughout my life I will honor them. Help me not to focus on their mistakes, but upon the good things they've shared with me. Through your grace I will listen to my father's instructions and never forsake my mother's teaching. Thank you for them, Father.

Lord, I want to be a wise child of my parents, one who brings joy to them. May my father and mother be glad because of me, and may my mother rejoice over me.

Help me to bless my parents in as many ways as possible. I will rise up and call my mother blessed. Thank you for her compassion for me, and thank you for the discipline I've received from my parents. I appreciate their love in my life.

Thank you for imparting your righteousness to me, Father. I want my life to always bring joy to my parents. Help me to walk in your wisdom, Father, that I would be a delight to my parents. Thank you for showing me the importance of obeying my parents in you, Lord, for this is right to do. I thank you for the promise you've given to those who honor their father and mother, that it would be well with us and that we may live long on the Earth.

I love my parents, Father, and I thank you for them. Bless them with every spiritual blessing in heavenly places in Christ.

In Jesus name I pray, Amen.

Scriptures: Exodus 20:12; Proverbs 1:8; Proverbs 10:1; Proverbs 23:25; Proverbs 31:26–31; Psalm 103:13; Proverbs 3:11-12; Proverbs 23:24; Ephesians 1:3.

Personal Affirmation: From this point forward I will honor and serve my parents with gladness, because I know they deserve both kindness and respect from me.

Reflection: *"There is no friendship, no love, like that of the parent for the child"* (Henry Ward Beecher).

PART V

PRAYERS THAT CHANGE THINGS IN YOUR CHURCH RELATIONSHIPS

Chapter 1

YOUR RELATIONSHIP WITH YOUR PASTOR

*Remember them which have the rule over you,
who have spoken unto you the word of God.*

(Hebrews 13:7)

Central Focus: I have a responsibility to my pastor as much as he has a responsibility to me. My responsibility is to serve, encourage, and help him in every possible way. I will pray for him every day.

Prayer: O God, my loving Father, thank you for my pastor who has taught your Word so faithfully to me and his congregation. Bless him and anoint his ministry afresh. I thank you for his willingness to watch over my soul. Help me to be in subjection to him and to pray for him faithfully. May he continue to shepherd the flock you've given to him, exercising oversight according to your will, Father.

Help me never to lose heart in doing good for him and the church, for in due time I know I shall reap if I do not grow weary. My pastor is worthy of double honor, Lord, because he works hard at preaching and teaching.

Thank you, Father, for giving me a pastor who serves according to your heart and feeds his congregation with knowledge and understanding. Help him to perfect the saints for the work of the ministry and the edifying of the Body of Christ, till we all come in the unity of the faith and of the knowledge of the Son of God, unto a perfect man, unto the measure of the stature of the fullness of Christ.

Help me to get to know my pastor and to esteem him highly in love for his work's sake. May I ever recognize his leadership, value him, and seek his counsel. Help me to show proper concern for his welfare and safety at all times. Help me to remember that my pastor is worthy of his reward.

It is exciting to know that I am a laborer together with my pastor, as God's husbandry and his building. Lord God, bless and keep my pastor, Make your face shine upon him and be gracious unto him. Lift up your countenance upon him and give him your peace.

Uphold him with your grace and peace, Father, and may he realize that you have already blessed him with every spiritual blessing in heavenly places in Christ. Give him the spirit of wisdom and revelation in the knowledge of Jesus Christ. May the eyes of his understanding be enlightened, that he may know the hope of your calling and the riches of the glory of your inheritance in the saints. Help him to know the exceeding greatness of your power to those who believe.

May he ever walk worthy of you unto all pleasing, being fruitful in every good work, and increasing in the knowledge of you. May he be strengthened with all might, according to your glorious power, unto all patience and longsuffering with joyfulness, giving thanks to you, Father.

May he never be ashamed of the Gospel of Jesus Christ, for it is your power unto salvation.

In Jesus' name I pray, Amen.

Scriptures: Hebrews 13:7; Romans 13:1; 1 Peter 5:2; Galatians 6; 9; 1 Timothy 5:17; Jeremiah 3:15; Ephesians 4:12-13; 1 Thessalonians 5:12-13; Luke 10:7; 1 Corinthians 3:9; Numbers 6:24-26; Ephesians 1:3; Ephesians 1:17-19; Colossians 1:10-12; Romans 1:16.

Personal Affirmation: I will support my pastor in every possible way.

Reflection: *"If the church wants a better pastor, it only needs to pray for the one it has"* (Anonymous).

Chapter 2

YOUR RELATIONSHIP WITH
YOUR FELLOW-BELIEVERS

Be ye therefore followers of God, as dear children.
(Ephesians 5:1)

Central Focus: My Abba-Father has adopted me into His wonderful family, and now I have brothers and sisters in Christ. It is my responsibility to walk in love toward my fellow-believers.

Prayer: Father, I thank you for my brothers and sisters in Christ. Help me to follow you in everything and to walk in love toward my fellow-believers. Therefore, I ask that you would help me to get rid of any bitterness, wrath, anger, and evil-speaking and to replace those things with kindness, tender-heartedness, and forgiveness, as you for Christ's sake have forgiven me.

As one of your elect children, I will put on bowels of mercies, kindness, humbleness of mind, meekness, and longsuffering, and I will forbear with others in the Body and walk in forgiveness toward my fellow-believers. And above all these things, I will put on love, which is the bond of perfection.

Help me, Lord God, to let your peace rule in my heart and to let the word of Christ dwell within me in all wisdom, teaching and admonishing others in Psalms and hymns and spiritual songs, singing with grace in my heart unto you. Through your grace, Father, I will do everything in the name of the Lord Jesus, giving thanks to you by Him.

Thank you for showing me that love is patient and kind. It is not arrogant nor does it envy others. It never behaves in an unseemly way and never seeks its own way. It is not easily provoked, and it never thinks evil thoughts. Love does not rejoice in iniquity; it rejoices in the truth. It bears all things, believes all things, hopes all things, and endures all things. I'm so thankful, Lord, that love never fails. Help me to share this love with all my brothers and sisters in Christ.

Help me, Father, never to do anything through strife or vainglory. In lowliness of mind, I will esteem my fellow-believers as being better than myself. I will be careful to help meet the needs of others. Father, I ask that you would let the mind of Christ be within me.

Thank you, Father, for showing me what is good and what you require of me: to do justly, to love mercy, and to walk humbly with you. This I will do through your marvelous grace.

In Jesus' name I pray, Amen.

Prayers: Ephesians 5:1; Ephesians 5:2; Ephesians 4:31-32; Colossians 4:12-13; Colossians 4:14-17; 1 Corinthians 13; Philippians 2:2-5; Micah 6:8.

Personal Application: God is my Father, and my fellow-believers are my siblings. I will love Him with all my heart, soul, mind, and strength, and I will love them as I love myself.

Reflection: *"Aloneness can lead to loneliness. God's preventative for loneliness is intimacy—meaningful, open, sharing relationships with one another. In Christ we have the capacity for the fulfilling sense of belonging which comes from intimate fellowship with God and with other believers"* (Neil T. Anderson).

Chapter 3

YOUR RELATIONSHIP WITH YOUR TEACHERS

A disciple is not above his teacher, but everyone when he is fully trained will be like his teacher.

(Luke 6:40 NKJV)

Central Focus: I am thankful for my teachers. I want to learn as much as possible from them.

Prayer: Heavenly Father, I thank you for my teachers. I would like to become like them as I grow in the grace and knowledge of my Lord Jesus Christ. My teachers are models of good works and they show integrity, dignity, and sound speech in their relationships with me. Help me to be like them, Father.

Thank you for the gifts you've given to me, Father. Help me to use them to serve others, including my teachers, as a good steward of your grace. Help me to do my best to present myself to you as one who is approved, a workman who has no need to ever be ashamed, because I've learned from my teachers how to rightly divide your Word.

It is my heart's desire, Father, to know wisdom and instruction, to understand words of insight, and to receive instruction in wise dealing, righteousness, justice, and equity. I want to give prudence to the simple and knowledge and discretion to youths. As I grow in your wisdom, Lord, through the work of my teachers, I know I will increase in learning and obtain guidance from you. Thank you, Father.

Keep me steadfast, immoveable, and always abounding in your work, O Lord, for I know that my labor is never in vain when it is in you. Help my teachers realize this, as well.

Help me always to fear you and to keep your commandments, for these are my primary duty. My teachers are faithfully dividing your Word, Father. Continue to bless them and anoint their ministry. They know your Word so well, and they understand that it has been inspired by you and it is profitable for teaching, reproof, for correction, and for training in righteousness.

They are teaching me to observe all that you have commanded, Father. Thank you for your promise to be with me unto the end of the age. I know my teachers take your Word very seriously, Father, and I'm very grateful for that.

Help me to build a constructive and long-lasting relationship with my teachers, Father. Help me to love them and serve them and to heed their instructions. They are helping to perfect your work in my life so that I will be able to do the work of the ministry for the edifying of your Body. At one time we will all come in the unity of the faith and of the knowledge of Jesus unto perfection and we will be granted the stature of the fullness of Christ.

As a result, I will no longer be tossed to and fro and carried about with every wind of doctrine by the sleight of men and cunning craftiness, but speaking the truth in love, I will grow up into Christ in all things. Thank you, Father.

Scriptures: Luke 6:40; 2 Peter 3:18; 1 Peter 4:10; 2 Timothy 2:15; Proverbs 1:1-33; 1 Corinthians 15:58; Ecclesiastes 12:12-13; 2 Timothy 3:16; Ephesians 4: 11-15.

Personal Affirmation: I resolve to be a good student, to learn all I can from my instructors, and to serve them in every way I can. I am very thankful for my teachers.

Reflection: *"The mediocre teacher tells. The good teacher explains. The superior teacher demonstrates. The great teacher inspires"* (William Arthur Ward).

Chapter 4

YOUR RELATIONSHIP WITH THE BODY OF CHRIST

*But speaking the truth in love, may grow up into
him in all things, which is the head, even Christ.
From whom the whole body fitly joined together
and compacted by that which every joint supplieth,
according to the effectual working in the measure
of every part, maketh increase of the body
unto the edifying of itself in love.*

(Ephesians 4:15–16)

Central Focus: I thank God that I am a member of the
Body of Christ. It is my desire to be joined ever closer
to my brothers and sisters in Christ. I want to do my
part effectually and faithfully.

Prayer: Father, help me to learn to speak the truth in
love. I want to grow up into Christ in all things, for
He is the Head of the Body of which I am a member.
Help me to fulfill my responsibilities as a member of
the Body of Christ. It is quite amazing to me to reflect
upon the fact that we are many members in one body.
We are so closely connected. Thank you, Father.

I thank you, Father, that you have made Christ to be
our Head. Help me to obey Him in all things. He is our
peace. He is bringing us together in unity and He has

147

reconciled us in one body by the Cross of Jesus Christ. Thank you, Father.

Help me to walk worthy of the vocation to which you have called me with all lowliness, meekness, and patience. Help me to forbear with my fellow-believers in love. I will endeavor always to maintain the unity of the Spirit in the bond of peace.

I realize, Father, that there is one Body, one Spirit, and one hope of my calling. There is one Lord, one faith, one baptism, and one God and Father of all. I thank you that you are above all, through all, and in all of us.

You have given to every one of us grace according to the measure of the stature of the fullness of the gift of Christ. Thank you for your grace, Father, and thank you for the ministerial gifts that are at work in your Body to perfect the saints and edify the Body of Christ. The goal is that we would all come in the unity of the faith and of the knowledge of your Son unto a perfect man, unto the measure of the stature of the fullness of Christ. Help me to do my part in this process, Father.

Henceforth, I shall not be tossed to and fro by every wind of doctrine or by the sleight of man and cunning craftiness. Speaking the truth in love, I will grow up into Him in all things. From Christ the whole body fitly joined together and compacted by that which every joint supplies, according to the effectual working in the measure of every part, makes increase of the Body unto the edifying of itself in love.

Help me to walk not as other Gentiles walk, in the vanity of their minds. I thank you that Christ has dispelled that kind of darkness from my life. I am being renewed in the spirit of my mind, and I am putting on the new man, which is being formed in righteousness and true holiness. Therefore, I will not lie, but I will speak truth with my fellow-believers, for we are members one of another.

I will be your follower, Father, and I will walk in love, as Christ has loved me and given himself for me. It is this that will strengthen my relationship with all members of the Body of Christ.

In Jesus' name I pray, Amen.

Scriptures: Ephesians 4:15-16; Romans 12:4-5; Ephesians 1: 22-23; Ephesians 2:14-16; Ephesians 4.

Personal Affirmation: As a member of the Body of Christ, I will do my part to edify the Body in love and to serve my fellow-believers. I want to have a more intimate fellowship with them.

Reflection: *"The true Church can never fail, for it is based upon a Rock"* (T.S. Eliot).

PART VI

PRAYERS THAT CHANGE YOUR RELATIONSHIP WITH YOURSELF

Chapter 1

A PRAYER FOR EMOTIONAL HEALTH

And ye shall know the truth, and the truth shall make you free.

(John 8:32)

Central Focus: God wants me to be whole in every part of my being—emotionally, physically, and spiritually.

Prayer: O God, help me to know the truth about myself, for I know this will make me free. I believe your promise that you will heal my broken-heartedness and bind up my wounds. Thank you, Father.

I ask you to restore emotional health to me. Restore my soul and restore to me the joy of my salvation. Thank you for being my Shepherd. Because you are, I know I shall never want for anything. Make me to lie down in green pastures and lead me beside the still waters. Lead me in the paths of righteousness for your name's sake. Even when I am walking through the shadow of death, I will fear no evil, for I know you are with me. Your rod and your staff bring me great comfort. Thank you for preparing a table before me in the presence of my enemies. Anoint my head with oil. My cup overflows. Surely goodness and mercy shall follow me all the days of my life, and I shall dwell in your house forever. Thank you, Father.

Bring me out of prison, that I may give thanks to your name! I know the righteous will surround me, and you will deal bountifully with me. As I draw near to you, I know you are drawing near to me. I know that you will never leave me nor forsake me. Indeed, you will be with me until the end of the age.

I will hope continually, Father, and I will praise you more and more. How I thank you for your joy, which is my strength. Jesus said, "Come unto me, all ye that labour and are heavy laden, and I will give you rest." I do so now, and I thank you for the rest you have provided for me.

Because of your mercies to me, Father, I now present my body to you as a living sacrifice, holy and acceptable unto you, for I know this is my reasonable service to you. I will not be conformed to this world any longer. Instead, I will be transformed by the renewing of my mind, that I will be able to prove what your good, perfect, and acceptable will is. Renew my mind, Father.

In Jesus' name I pray, Amen.

Scriptures: John 8:32; Psalm 147:3; Jeremiah 30:17; Psalm 23:3; Psalm 51:12; Psalm 23; Psalm 142:7; James 4:8; Hebrews 13:5; Matthew 28;20; Psalm 71:14; Nehemiah 8:10; Matthew 11:28; Romans 12:1-2.

Personal Application: God's Word shows me how to walk in emotional health. The truth has made me free.

Therefore, I will stand fast in the liberty wherewith Christ has set me free, and I will not be entangled with any yoke of bondage. (See Galatians 5:1.)

Reflection: *"When circumstances seem impossible, when all signs of grace in you seem at their lowest ebb, when temptation is fiercest, when love and joy and hope seem well-nigh extinguished in your heart, then rest, without feeling and without emotion, in the Father's faithfulness"* (D. Tryon).

Chapter 2

LOVING YOURSELF

He that getteth wisdom loveth his own soul:
he that keepeth understanding shall find good.
(Proverbs 19:8)

Central Focus: Realizing that I am to love God, others, and myself, I seek to learn how to love myself more fully and in ways that will be good for me.

Prayer: My loving Father, help me to get wisdom. As I do so, I know that I will have a renewed sense of healthy self-love. Therefore, I seek your grace to help me be patient with myself, for I know you are not finished with me. Help me to avoid all arrogance, pride, and selfishness. Keep me from being irritable or resentful. Give me a fuller measure of your love, which bears all things, believes all things, hopes all things, and endures all things. Help me to apply these truths to myself as well as others.

With your help I will be an example to the believers in speech, conduct, love, faith, and purity, and I know this will help me to respect myself and love myself in a healthy way. Thank you for purchasing me with the price of Jesus' blood. Because this is true, I will glorify you in my body, Father.

I will do my best to present myself to you as one approved, a worker who never needs to be ashamed, rightly handling your Word of truth. I am crucified with Christ. It is no longer I who live, but Christ who lives in me. And the life I now live I live in the flesh I live by faith in the Son of God, who loved me and gave himself for me. Thank you for Jesus, Father.

Thank you for the faith you've imparted to me. Because I am born of you, Father, I am able to overcome the world. It is faith that is the victory that overcomes the world. Thank you for making me into a new creation, Lord. The old has passed away and all things have become new in my life.

How I praise you for your grace which has enabled me to put off the old self with all its heinous practices and to put on the new self, which is being renewed in knowledge after your image. I will walk in a manner that is worthy of the calling to which I've been called, with all humility and gentleness and with patience. I will bear with others in love.

Father, help me to trust in you with all my heart without leaning on my own understanding. In all my ways I will acknowledge you, and I know you will direct my paths. Praise your mighty name!

In Jesus' name, Amen.

Scriptures: Proverbs 19:8; 1 Corinthians 13; 1 Timothy 4:12; 2 Timothy 2:15; Galatians 2:20; 1 John 5:4; 2 Corinthians 5:17; Ephesians 4:1-2; Proverbs 3:5-6.

Personal Affirmation: God is enabling me to love myself with a healthy love. Because this is true, I can now love Him and others more fully.

Reflection: *"When people believe in themselves, they have the first secret of success"* (Norman Vincent Peale).

Chapter 3

STRENGTHENING YOUR FAITH

But they that wait upon the Lord shall renew their strength; they shall mount up with wings as eagles; they shall run and not be weary; and they shall walk and not faint.

(Isaiah 40:31)

Central Focus: Faith in God helps me to accept myself, love myself, and respect myself. His faith is imparted to me through His Word. (See Romans 10:17.)

Prayer: Father, help me to strengthen my faith through your Word, which is a lamp unto my feet and a light unto my path. In so doing, I know I shall renew my strength and mount up with wings as eagles. Thank you, Father.

I present all my cares and worries to you, Lord. Thank you for always thinking about me and watching over me. Through your grace I will not let my heart be troubled, and I will not fear, for I know you have given me peace—not a fragile kind of peace like the world gives, but lasting peace of mind and heart.

Thank you for showing me that I do not have to worry about anything. Instead, I will pray to you, tell you my needs, and thank you for your provision in my life.

As a result, I experience your wonderful peace that surpasses all understanding. Your peace will guard my heart and my mind through Christ Jesus.

Without you I can do nothing, but through you I can do all things. Thank you for your promise to supply all my needs according to your riches in glory by Christ Jesus. I waited patiently for you, Lord God. Thank you for listening and hearing my cry. You lifted me out of the pit of despair and set my feet on the solid rock. Thank you for giving me a new song, a song of praise to you. I praise you that many will now hear of the glorious things you've done for me, standing in awe of you, and putting their trust in you.

Yes, you hear me when I pray. Thank you, Father, for saving me out of all my troubles. Thank you for being close to me and for rescuing me. I know you will always help me.

Help me to be strong and courageous and not to fear. I know you are with me and you will never leave me nor forsake me. Hallelujah!

You are my hiding place from all of life's storms. Thank you for keeping me from getting into trouble and surrounding me with songs of victory. Thank you for instructing me and guiding me along the right pathway.

I choose to trust in you, Father, and I know you will keep me in perfect peace. I will trust in you always, for you are my everlasting strength. As you strengthen my faith, I am able to rest in you and wait patiently for you to act. Because you are on my side, Father, nothing can ever be against me. Thank you for holding my right hand, Lord. I am no longer afraid. You are helping me.

It's wonderful to know that you are fighting my battles for me. Therefore, I do not need to fight. I can simply take my place, stand quietly, and watch you at work in my behalf. I will not be afraid or discouraged. Thank you, Father.

Thank you for strengthening my faith. In Jesus' name I pray, Amen.

Scriptures: Romans 10:17; Psalm 119:105; Isaiah 40:31; 1 Peter 5:7; John 14:27; Philippians 4:6-7; John 15:5; Philippians 4:13; Philippians 4:19; Psalm 40:1-3; Psalm 34:17-19; Deuteronomy 31:6; Psalm 32:7-9; Isaiah 26:3-4; Psalm 37:7; Romans 8:31-32; Isaiah 41:13-14; 2 Chronicles 20:17.

Personal Affirmation: Faith is the victory that overcomes the world. Therefore, I will walk by faith and not by sight. I will let the word of faith be on my lips. I will speak forth God's Word.

Reflection: *"It is the heart that feels God, not the reason; this is faith"* (Blaise Pascal).

Chapter 4

SELF-ESTEEM

*I will praise thee; for I am fearfully
and wonderfully made.*
(Psalm 139:14)

Central Focus: I am a person of value. God created me in His image. Jesus Christ died for me. God has given me important things to do.

Prayer: Thank you for your Word, Father, which shows that I am to esteem myself because I know you esteem me. Indeed, I am fearfully and wonderfully made. I am one of your marvelous works. You formed my inward parts and knitted me together in my mother's womb. I praise you, Father.

In your sight, dear God, the important thing is not outward appearances, for you look on the heart. Therefore, I choose to have a gentle and quiet spirit, which I know you find very precious in your sight.

Thank you for telling me that I am precious to you, Father. Thank you for your love. I know you have great plans for my life, plans for welfare and not for evil to give me a future and a hope. I believe this, Lord, and I thank you for it.

I know you are with me wherever I go, and because this

is true, I will be strong and courageous. I will neither be frightened nor dismayed. Your love amazes me, Father, because it is through your love for me that I am now your child. Hallelujah!

I thank you that I am your workmanship, created in Christ Jesus for good works, which you have prepared beforehand. Help me to walk in them. I am a part of your chosen race, a royal priesthood, a holy nation, and a people for your possession. I will proclaim your excellence. Thank you for calling me out of darkness, into your marvelous light.

I know that you know the numbers of hairs on my head, and you have told me that I am of more value than many sparrows. Thank you, Father.

Because you are for me, Lord, I do not need to worry about anyone who may be against me. Nothing shall be able to separate me from your love. Thank you for your willingness to give me so many great things. I can do all things through Christ who strengthens me.

You are in our midst, Lord God, and you are the mighty One who will save. Thank you for rejoicing over me with gladness, quieting me with your love, and exulting over me with singing. I love you, Lord.

In Jesus' name I pray, Amen.

Scriptures: Psalm 139:14; 1 Samuel 16:7; 1 Peter 3:3-4; Isaiah 43:4; Jeremiah 29:11; Joshua 1:9; 1 John 3:1; Ephesians 2:10; 1 Peter 2:9; Luke 12:7; Romans 8:31-39; Philippians 4:13; Zephaniah 3:17.

Personal Affirmation: I am learning to value myself because I know God values me. What a wonderful realization this is!

Reflection: *"No one can make you feel inferior without your consent"* (Eleanor Roosevelt).

Chapter 5

CONFIDENCE

For the Lord shall be thy confidence, and shall keep they foot from being taken.

(Proverbs 3:26)

Central Focus: The closer I get to God, the more confident I become.

Prayer: Dear Father, I thank you that you are my confidence. In you I find all that I need. The closer I get to you, I learn to respect you and in this I find strong confidence. Thank you for being my place of refuge.

My confidence is not in myself, not in my flesh, but totally in you, Lord. This is true confidence, and I thank you for it.

My heart does not condemn me, Lord, and because this is true, all my confidence is in you. I am confident that you will give me what I ask from you, because I endeavor to keep your commandments and do things that are pleasing in your sight.

Thank you for imparting faith to me, Father, for it is my faith that gives me confidence, because it is the substance of things hoped for and the evidence of things not seen. You are my hope, O Lord God. You have been my trust since I was young.

I am happy because I have made you my trust. I will not place my trust in human beings. I am happy because I have the God of Jacob for my help. All my hope is in you, O Lord, my God, for you are the One who made Heaven and Earth, the sea, and all that is therein and you keep truth forever. Praise your holy name!

I glory in you, Father, for you are the Lord who constantly exercises loving-kindness, judgment, and righteousness. Thank you, Lord. I do not put confidence in the flesh or on outward privileges and external appearances. Instead, I put my confidence in Jesus Christ, and I glory in Him.

With your help, holy Father, I know I can advance against a troop and I can scale a wall! I am determined and confident. I am not afraid or discouraged, for you are with me wherever I go. Thank you, Father. My heart is fixed, O God, my heart is steadfast and confident. Because of this, I will sing and make melody.

Thank you for guarding me and keeping me in perfect and constant peace because my mind is stayed on you. I commit myself to you, I lean on you instead of on my own understanding, and I hope confidently in you.

In quietness and trusting confidence I find great strength. Thank you for making me into a confident person.

In Jesus' name I pray, Amen.

Scriptures: Proverbs 3:26; Proverbs 14:26; Philippians 3:3-4; 1 John 3:21; Hebrews 11:1; Psalm 71:5; Psalm 40:4;

Jeremiah 9:23-24; Philippians 3:3; Psalm 18:29; Joshua 1:9; Psalm 57:7; Isaiah 30:15.

Personal Affirmation: I am a confident person, because God is my confidence and my strength. I will not fear but go forth in confidence. I am God-confident, not self-confident.

Reflection: *"Aerodynamically the bumblebee shouldn't be able to fly, but the bumblebee doesn't know that, so it goes on flying anyway"* (Mary Kay Ash).

Chapter 6

FREEDOM

*Stand fast therefore in the liberty wherewith Christ
hath made us free, and be not entangled again
with the yoke of bondage.*

(Galatians 5:1)

Central Focus: When we know and live by the truth,
we shall be free indeed.

Prayer: Heavenly Father, thank you for the spiritual
freedom you've given to me. Help me to stand fast in
that freedom and never again to be entangled with
the yoke of bondage. Thank you for sending Jesus to
bind up the broken-hearted, to proclaim liberty to the
captives, and to open the prison doors of all who are
bound. I praise you, Father, for the freedom He gives
to me. Truly, I am free indeed!

I will live in freedom, because I want to follow you in all
things. Thank you for sending the Holy Spirit. Where He
is, there is freedom. Enable me to walk in the Spirit at
all times so that I would not fulfill the lusts of my flesh.

Father, I thank you that there is no longer any
condemnation within me, for the law of the Spirit of
life in Christ Jesus has set me free from the law of sin
and death. Thank you for calling me to freedom, Lord.

Help me to use the freedom you've given to me not as an opportunity to serve my flesh, but through love to serve others.

I thank you that you have set me free from the bondage to corruption, because you've given me the glorious liberty that all your children know. Thank you for leading me by your Holy Spirit.

Father, you are my refuge and my strength, a very present help in times of trouble. Thank you for always being there for me.

Thank you for sending Jesus who came to give me abundant life. Without Him I can do nothing, but through Him I can do all things. Help me to abide in Christ, for I know this is what brings freedom to me. I will abide in Him and let His words abide in me. Then I know I will receive from you what I ask. Thank you, Father.

I want to glorify you, Father, by bearing much fruit for you. Let your freedom flow forth from me, so that others will want to know you.

In Jesus' name I pray, Amen.

Scriptures: Galatians 5:1; Isaiah 61:1-3; John 8:36; Psalm 119:45; 2 Corinthians 3:17; Galatians 5:16; Romans 8:1; Romans 8:21; Psalm 46:1; John 10:10; John 15:5; Philippians 4:13; John 15:7; John 15:*.

Personal Affirmation: I will walk in freedom from this point on. The pathway to freedom is paved with love, faith, and righteousness. I am free from all anxiety, fear, confusion, and discouragement.

Reflection: *"Hallowed be Thy name,* not mine, *Thy kingdom come,* not mine, *Thy will be done,* not mine, *Give us peace with Thee, peace with men, peace with ourselves, and free us from all fear"* (Dag Hammarskjold).

Chapter 7

VICTORY

Nay, in all these things we are more than conquerors through him that loved us.

(Romans 8:37)

Central Focus: The victory God gives to me always puts me on the winning side.

Prayer: O God, my heavenly Father, thank you for the victory you have given to me. I can honestly say that I am more than a conqueror through Jesus Christ, my Lord. To you, O God, belongs the greatness and the might, the glory, the victory, the majesty, the splendor. Yes, everything in Heaven and everything on Earth is yours! You are high above all this, and riches and honor come from you. I thank you that you are the Ruler over all. You hold strength and power in the palm of your hand to build up and give strength to all. Therefore, I give thanks to you and I praise your splendid name.

Faith is the victory that overcomes the world. Strengthen my faith, Lord God, through your Word, which is a lamp unto my feet and a light unto my path. I believe your Word, and I know that you will accomplish what I ask for through faith. Help me to live by faith and not by sight, because I know this is a great key to victory in my life.

Through your grace and power I will fight the good fight of faith and take hold of the eternal life to which I was called when I made a good confession in the presence of many witnesses. I know this is a fight I will win because of you, Father.

I draw near to you with a sincere heart that is in the full assurance of faith. My heart has been sprinkled clean from a guilty conscience. My body has been washed with pure water. I take my stand upon your promises, Father, because I know they will keep me going and lead me to victory. Thank you for always keeping your Word to me.

With your help I will be strong and courageous. I will not let anything intimidate me. You are going ahead of me, Father, and I know you won't let me down or ever leave me. Thank you so much for making me your victorious servant.

How I praise you, Father, that nothing shall ever be able to separate me from your love, which is in Christ Jesus, my Lord.

In Jesus' name I pray, Amen.

Scriptures: Romans 8:37; 1 Chronicles 29:11; 1 John 5:4-5; Psalm 119:105; Mark 11:23; 2 Corinthians 5:7; 1 Timothy 6:12; Deuteronomy 3:16.

Personal Affirmation: I will maintain the victory Jesus has given to me at all time. I will be vigilant as I fight the good fight of faith. God will never leave me nor forsake me, and He will fight my battles for me.

Reflection: *"The smile of God is victory"* (John Greenleaf Whittier).

Chapter 8

OVERCOMING GUILT AND SHAME

There is therefore now no condemnation to them which are in Christ Jesus.

(Romans 8:1)

Central Focus: Through Christ I'm free from the fear of the future and the guilt of the past.

Prayer: Thank you, Father-God, for taking all condemnation from me. I have confessed my sins to you, and I know you are faithful and just to forgive my sins and to cleanse me from all unrighteousness.

Realizing that no temptation has overtaken me that is not common to others and that you are completely faithful to me, I know you will not allow me to be tempted above my ability, but you will provide a way of escape for me, that I will be able to endure it. Thank you, Father.

I can do all things through Christ who strengthens me. Thank you for having compassion on me, Father, and for treading my iniquities underfoot. I praise you for the knowledge that you have cast all my sins into the depths of the deepest sea.

I believe in you, Father, and in your Word, which contains

so many wonderful promises for me. Because I believe in you, I know all guilt and shame are gone. Thank you, Father.

How I praise you for not restraining your mercy from me. I know your steadfast love and faithfulness will ever preserve me. It's thrilling to know that you are writing your laws on my heart and mind, and you will no longer remember my sins and lawless deeds.

Therefore, laying aside every weight and the sin that does so easily beset me, I will run with perseverance the race that you've set before me, looking unto Jesus who is the Author and Finisher of my faith.

Blessed are you, O God, the Father of my Lord Jesus Christ. Thank you for blessing me with all spiritual blessings in the heavenly places in Christ. Those wonderful blessings include your love, your grace, your forgiveness, your strength, your justification, your joy, your redemption, and your mercy. I feel very privileged to have such a glorious inheritance, Father.

Thank you for the exceeding greatness of your power toward me, O Father. It is a power that has wiped away all my guilt and shame.

In Jesus' name I pray, Amen.

Scriptures: Romans 8:1; 1 John 1:9; 1 Corinthians 10:13; Philippians 4:13; Micah 7:19; John 3:18; Psalm 40:11–12; Hebrews 10:15–18; Ephesians 1:3; Ephesians 1:19.

Personal Affirmation: All guilt and shame are gone

from my life. My sins have been buried in the depths of the deepest sea.

Reflection: *"Guilt is the teacher; love is the lesson"* (Joan Borysenko).

PART VII

PRAYERS THAT CHANGE THINGS IN YOUR COMMUNITY AND WORK RELATIONSHIPS

Chapter 1

YOUR RELATIONSHIP WITH YOUR ENEMIES

But I say unto you, Love your enemies,
bless them that curse you, do good to them that
hate you, and pray for them which despitefully use
you, and persecute you.

(Matthew 5:44)

Central Focus: As I let God arise in my life, I know my enemies will be scattered. (See Psalm 68:1.) No weapon that is formed against me shall prosper. (See Isaiah 54:17.)

Prayer: Heavenly Father, I thank you for all the promises of your Word, which are Yes and Amen in Christ Jesus. Help me to believe the words of Jesus and to act upon the words of Jesus who tells me to love my enemies, bless those who curse me, do good to them that hate me, and pray for them which despitefully use me. Help me to do these things faithfully, Father.

I surrender my right to self-defense to you, Lord. I want you to arise in my life, and I know this will scatter my enemies. Thank you for your promise that no weapon that is formed against me shall prosper, and that you will condemn those tongues that judge me, for this is my heritage as one of your servants. Thank you, Father.

In the day of trouble you will keep me safe in your dwelling, Father. Thank you for this promise. You will hide me in the shelter of your tabernacle and set me high upon a rock. Then my head will be exalted above the enemies who surround me. In your tabernacle I will sacrifice with shouts of joy. I will sing and make music to you, Lord.

Through you I will gain the victory over my enemies, Father, and I know you will trample them down. I love you, Lord, and I hate evil. Thank you for guarding me and delivering me from the hands of the wicked.

My heart is secure in you. I have no fear, for I know I will look in triumph on my enemies. You are always with me, and you are my Helper. Thank you, Father.

Thank you for going with me to fight for me against my enemies. I know you will give me the victory over them. I worship you, Father, and, as I do so, I know you will deliver me from my enemies. You are my constant Helper. I will not be afraid. What can man do to me?

Trusting you every step of the way, I will not give place to the devil, and I will not let any corrupt communication proceed out of my mouth. I will not grieve the Holy Spirit of God, because He has sealed me for the day of redemption. Help me to get rid of all bitterness, wrath, anger, clamor, and evil speaking. Show me how to be kind to others, including my enemies, to be tenderhearted and forgiving to all others, even as you have forgiven me for Christ's sake.

Help me to remember to walk in love toward all.

In Jesus' name I pray, Amen.

Scriptures: 2 Corinthians 1:20; Matthew 5:44; Psalm 68:1; Isaiah 54:17; Psalm 27:5; Psalm 27:6; Psalm 60:12; Psalm 97:10; Psalm 112:8; Psalm 118:7; Deuteronomy 20:4; Hebrews 13:6; Ephesians 4:26–32; Ephesians 5:2.

Personal Affirmation: I will endeavor to have no enemies in my life. However, there are times when people will go against me. At such times I will be loving and forgiving toward them.

Reflection: *"Always forgive your enemies; nothing annoys them so much"* (Oscar Wilde).

Chapter 2

YOUR RELATIONSHIP WITH YOUR FRIENDS

A friend loveth at all times,
and a brother is born for adversity.
(Proverbs 17:17)

Central Focus: Being thankful for my friends, I will love them at all times. I will pray for them on a regular basis, asking God to bless them and meet their every need.

Prayer: O God, my Father, thank you for my friends. Help me to love them at all times and to help them in every way I can. In the same way that Jonathan and David loved each other, I want to make a solemn pact with each of my friends.

Help me to give godly advice to my friends. May I never spread gossip about my friends, for I know this will separate us.

I want to be always loyal to my friends, and I want to always be there for them and to help them in their times of need. I want to be a true friend, one who sticks closer than a brother to my friends. I will be a true and reliable friend to them.

Help me not to befriend the wrong kind of people, those who are angry and hot-tempered, for I know the danger is that I might become like them if I am with them a lot.

Help me not to be afraid to rebuke my friends, for I know that wounds from a sincere friend are better than many kisses from an enemy. I want to give heartfelt counsel to my friends, sweet counsel that is like perfume and incense.

Father, I know that iron sharpens iron, and I want my friendships to have that quality. May I sharpen my friends as I build on my relationships with them. I know that two people are better than one, for they help each other succeed. If one person falls, the other can reach out and help. A person who falls alone can be in very serious trouble. Likewise, two people lying together can keep each other warm, but such warmth is not available to someone who is lying alone. A person standing alone can be attacked and defeated, but two can stand back-to-back and conquer. Three are even better, for a triple-braided cord is not easily broken. Father, I pray that this would be descriptive of all my friendships.

Help me to be the kind of friend who loves so much that he is willing to lay down his life for his friends. Thank you, Father, for the friendship I have with the Lord Jesus Christ, who has called me His friend. I deeply enjoy my friendship with you, Father, which you restored to me through the death of your Son.

In Jesus' name I pray, Amen.

Scriptures: Proverbs 17:17; 1 Samuel 18:1-3; Proverbs 12:26; Proverbs 16:28; Proverbs 17:17; Proverbs 18:24; Proverbs 20:6; Proverbs 22:24-25; Proverbs 27:5-6; Proverbs 27:9; Proverbs 27:17; Ecclesiastes 4:9-12; John 15:13-15; Romans 5:10.

Personal Affirmation: I need my friends and I am thankful for them. I commit myself to being a true, loving friend to each one.

Reflection: *"A good friend is a connection to life, a tie to the past, a road to the future, the key to sanity in a totally insane world"* (Lois Wyse).

Chapter 3

YOUR RELATIONSHIP WITH YOUR BOSS

Let every soul be subject unto the higher powers.
For there is no power but of God:
the powers that be are ordained of God.

(Romans 13:1-4)

Central Focus: I want an effective relationship with my boss. I need to respect him or her, honor him or her, and help him or her to be successful.

Prayer: Heavenly Father, help me to realize that my boss has been put in his position through your power and authority. Therefore, I respect him or her and honor him or her. Help me to have the right attitude toward him or her at all times.

With your help, Father, I will faithfully do what my boss asks me to do at all times, unless, of course, he or she asks me to do something wrong. Let me serve him or her in the same way that I serve and honor Christ.

Help me to count him or her as being worthy of honor, that your name and doctrine would not be blasphemed. Help me to maintain good works in my employment, because doing so is good and profitable for all.

I will hold fast the faithful Word, as I have been taught.

I am thankful for my job, Father, because I know that it is my responsibility and it enables me to provide for my own needs and those of my family.

Help me to view my boss as your servant and my teacher, Father. I want to serve him or her and help him or her in every possible way.

As one of your elect children, I will put on the new man, which is renewed in knowledge after your image. I will put on bowels of mercies, kindness, humbleness of mind, meekness, and longsuffering (patience) in the workplace.

Help me to forbear with my boss and my co-workers. Even as Christ has forgiven me, I will forgive and accept them. Help me to walk in love toward my boss and my co-workers.

In Jesus' name I pray, Amen.

Scriptures: Romans 13:1-14; Ephesians 6:5-8; 1 Timothy 6:1-2; Titus 3:8; Titus 1:9; 1 Timothy 5:8; Romans 13:4.

Personal Affirmation: I resolve to be a diligent employee and to give appropriate honor and respect to my boss.

Reflection: *"If you are having difficulty loving or relating to an individual, take him to God. Bother the Lord with this person. Don't you be bothered with him—leave him at the throne"* (Charles Swindoll).

Chapter 4

YOUR RELATIONSHIPS WITH YOUR CO-WORKERS

Walk worthy of the vocation wherewith ye are called, with all lowliness and meekness, with longsuffering, forbearing one another in love.

(Ephesians 4:1-2)

Central Focus: It is my desire to be a godly example in front of my co-workers. They need to see the truth of the gospel exhibited in my life.

Prayer: Heavenly Father, thank you for my job and my co-workers. Help me to walk worthy of the vocation to which you've called me in front of them. I want to exhibit lowliness, meekness, patience, and love toward them.

Love is patient, kind, and not jealous. Love does not brag and is not arrogant. Love does not behave unbecomingly, and it does not seek its own. Love is not easily provoked, does not take into account a wrong suffered, and does not rejoice in unrighteousness. Instead, it always rejoices in the truth, bears all things, believes all things, hopes all things, and endures all things. Love never fails. Help me to walk in this kind of love every day on the job.

Father, help me to stimulate others to practice love and good deeds. Help me to encourage my co-workers. Help me, Father, to be an example of the believers in word, conversation, charity, spirit, faith, and purity.

Help me to remember that the natural man cannot receive the things of your Spirit, Father, for they are spiritually discerned.

In my dealings with my co-workers, I ask you to enable me to do justly, love mercy, and walk humbly with you. May they see you in my life.

Help me to never forget your Word, Father. I will keep your commandments. Let not mercy and truth leave me. As I walk in your ways, I will find favor and good understanding in the sight of my co-workers and you. Thank you, Father.

Through your grace, I will walk in wisdom in front of my co-workers. I know you will be my confidence, Father. May I never withhold good from those to whom it is due, when it is within my power to do it. Show me how I can help my co-workers, and never to strive with them. May I never envy them.

Bless my co-workers in every way, Father, and supply their needs according to your riches in glory by Christ Jesus in whose name I pray, Amen.

Scriptures: Ephesians 4:1-2; 1 Corinthians 13; Hebrews 10:24-25; 1 Timothy 4:12; 1 Corinthians 2:14; Micah 6:8; Proverbs 3:1-3; Philippians 4:19.

Personal Affirmation: I want to be a blessing to my co-workers. Therefore, I commit myself to praying for them and helping them.

Reflection: *"Remember, we all stumble, every one of us. That's why it's a comfort to go hand in hand"* (Emily Kimbrough).

Part VIII

Bible Blessings for Your Relationships

Chapter 1

Bible Blessing for My Child

Train up a child in the way he should go, and when he is old he will not depart from it.
(Proverbs 22:6, NKJV)

Central Focus: I love my child, and I will always want the best for him or her. God's everlasting love will always be with him or her.

Prayer: Father-God, I thank you and praise you for my precious child, _____.
Bless him or her at all times and in every way, and help me to be a joyful parent to him or her. Thank you for this precious gift from your hands.

Help me always to cherish _____
as an inheritance I've received from you, Father, and help me never to forget that he or she is not my possession. Thank you for creating him or her for your purposes. I praise you for the glory of your creation that I see in my child, for it is clear to me that he or she is fearfully and wonderfully made and all your works are marvelous.

Keep me from ever provoking him or her to wrath, Father, and help me to remember your mandate to bring him or her up in your nurture and admonition. I will do so with your help, my Father.

Keep my child from all evil, Father, and give your angels charge over him or her. Protect him or her and lead him or her in the paths of righteousness for your name's sake. Help change to remember you in the days of his or her youth, while the evil days are not near. May he or she always be a good example of the believers in every way.

I bless my child, Father, even as Jesus blessed the little children that came to Him. Keep him or her in the center of your will. Help him or her to discover your calling at an early age, as he or she surrenders his or her will to you for salvation and eternal life.

Help me, also, Lord God, to discover your calling on his or her life so that the training I provide for him or her will always contribute to the fulfillment of the purposes for which you created him or her. Help both of us to comprehend that he or she is your workmanship, created in Christ Jesus unto good works, which you have ordained for him or her to walk in, and that it is as _____ finds and walks in those good works that he or she will experience true joy, fulfillment, and blessing.

May my rejoicing always be centered on the trust that my child will always walk in the truth, because this is your commandment, Father. Indeed, Jesus is the way, the truth, and the life, and no one can come to you except they do so through Him. Help my child to realize this foundational truth throughout his or her life.

In the name of Jesus Christ I pray, Amen.

Scriptures: Psalm 113:9; Psalm 127:3; Psalm 139:14; Ephesians 6:4; John 17:15; Psalm 91:11; Psalm 23:3; Ecclesiastes 12:1; 1 Timothy 4:12; Matthew 19:14; John 3:16; Proverbs 22:6; Jeremiah 29:11; Ephesians 2:10; John 13:17; 2 John 4; John 14:6; John 16:24.

Personal Affirmation: With God's help, I will be an effective parent who loves and nurtures my child in the right way.

Reflection: *"Children are great imitators. So give them something great to imitate"* (Anonymous).

Chapter 2

BIBLE BLESSING FOR MY HUSBAND

Husbands, love your wives, just as Christ also loved the church and gave Himself for her that He might sanctify and cleanse her with the washing of water by the word.

(Ephesians 5:22-26, NKJV)

Central Focus: God gave me a wonderful husband, and I will cherish, honor, love, and serve him throughout my life.

Prayer: Father-God, thank you for my precious husband, and thank you for Jesus, who loves His Church so much that He gave himself for it. I ask you to show my husband how to love me as Jesus loves His Church—completely, sacrificially, and eternally. Bless him abundantly from your storehouse in Heaven.

Command your blessing to be upon him, Father, and upon all that he sets his hand to do. Establish him as a holy man of God, I pray.

Help me to see my role as his wife and helpmeet for what it truly is—a sacred calling. Continue your workmanship in my life, that my husband's heart will learn to safely trust in me and in you. May I do him good and not evil all the days of my life.

May I never give my husband any reason to grow bitter toward me, Father. Help us to reverence and honor each other, so we might be heirs together of the grace of life and our prayers will not be hindered.

Bless our marriage, Father. May we ever live each for the other and both for you. Keep us together always, as we endeavor to serve you by praying and working together. I pray that he would prosper in all things and be in health, just as his soul prospers in you.

May he never walk in the counsel of the ungodly, stand in the path of sinners, or sit in the seat of the scornful. Instead, may his delight ever be in your law, O Lord God, and may he meditate in your law both night and day, so he will become like a tree that is planted by the rivers of water, bringing forth his fruit in his season. Grant, dear God, that whatever he does will prosper.

Help my husband to always to put his trust in you, Father. May he learn to trust you with all his heart, without leaning on his own understanding. I pray that he would acknowledge you in all his ways and that you would always direct his paths. Thank you, Father.

Give my husband his heart's desires, O God, and do not withhold the requests of his lips. Meet him with the blessing of goodness, and set a crown of pure gold upon his head. Give him good health and longevity, I pray.

Bless him forever and make him exceedingly glad

about your presence in his life, dear Father. Help him to delight in doing your will at all times, and may he keep your Word as a treasure within his heart.

I pray that my husband would find all his strength in you, Father. Let your joy be his everlasting strength. Be his sun and shield, and give him grace and glory. Help him ever to remember that you will never withhold any good thing from him, as he walks uprightly before you.

Father, I thank you for hearing and answering my prayer of blessing for my husband.

In the blessed name of Jesus I pray, Amen.

Scriptures: Ephesians 5:22-26; Deuteronomy 28:12; Deuteronomy 28:8-9; Proverbs 31:11-12; Colossians 3:19; 1 Peter 3:7; 3 John 2; Psalm 1:1; Psalm 1:2-3; Proverbs 3:5-6; Psalm 21:2; Psalm 21:3; Psalm 21:4; Psalm 21:6; Psalm 40:8; Psalm 84:5; Nehemiah 8:10; Psalm 84:11; Jeremiah 33:3; John 16:24.

Personal Affirmation: My husband deserves all the respect, love, and devotion I can give. I choose to honor him by serving him, helping him, loving him, and blessing him.

Reflection: *"Many marriages would be better if the husband and the wife clearly understood that they are on the same side"* (Zig Ziglar).

Chapter 3

BIBLE BLESSING FOR MY WIFE

*Who can find a virtuous wife? For her worth is
far above rubies. The heart of her husband safely
trusts her; so he will have no lack of gain.*

(Proverbs 31:10-11, NKJV)

Central Focus: To love my wife as Christ loves His Church
means that I must love her without any reservations,
unconditionally, sacrificially, and eternally. Ours is an
unto-death-do-us-part relationship.

Prayer: Dear God, my heavenly Father, thank you for
my precious wife. I love her so much, and I ask you to
bless her abundantly out of your storehouse in Heaven.
Thank you for giving me a virtuous woman whose
worth is far above that of rubies.

Give me the grace to always trust her, Father, that she
will always do me good. Show my wife how to gird
herself with your strength, and let her experience the
fullness of your joy, which is her strength, all the days
of her life. I pray, mighty Father, that strength and honor
will be her clothing.

Bless my wife with wisdom, and may she always open
her mouth with the wisdom you impart to her. May
your law of kindness always be on her tongue, dear

Father. Help her to oversee the ways of our family and household.

Father, I want to bless her and call her blessed at all times. Show me how to do this more fully and effectively, as I let her know how excellent she is to me.

As my wife reverences me, may she always feel secure in my love for her. Help her to be reverent, self-controlled, and faithful in all things. Show her how to adorn her life with a meek and quiet spirit, which is of great price in your sight, dear God.

Bless my wife with the ability to trust you with all her heart, without leaning upon her own understanding. In all her ways may she acknowledge you, knowing that you will direct her paths.

It is my desire, Lord God, to rule my home well, to teach your precepts to my wife and children both through word and example, and always to endeavor to meet the needs of our family. Help me to bring up our children in the nurture and admonition of you, and to wash my wife in the water of your Word, even as Jesus has washed His bride, the Church.

Father, bless my wife with the certain knowledge that you are her refuge and strength, a very present help in times of trouble. Let your perfect love remove all fear from her heart, mind, and life. Help her to establish our home in wisdom, to find her confidence in you.

Thank you for hearing and answering this prayer of blessing for my wife.

In the holy name of Jesus I pray, Amen.

Scriptures: Deuteronomy 28:12; Proverbs 31:10; Proverbs 31:11-12; Proverbs 31:17; Nehemiah 8:10; Proverbs 31:25; James 1:5; Proverbs 31:26; Proverbs 31:27; Proverbs 31:28; Proverbs 31:29; Esther 1:20; 1 Timothy 3:11; 1 Peter 3:4; Proverbs 3:5-6; 1 Timothy 3:12; Deuteronomy 6:6-7; Ephesians 6:4; Ephesians 5:26-27; Psalm 91:1; Psalm 46:1; 1 John 4:18; Proverbs 14:1; Proverbs 14:26.

Personal Affirmation: My wife is the most wonderful woman I've ever known. She is very precious to me, and I will take good care of her for as long as I live.

Reflection: *"If ever two were one, then surely we. If ever man were loved by wife, then thee"* (Anne Bradstreet).

Prayers That Change Things
Pray God's Word— Get His Answers
by Lloyd Hildebrand

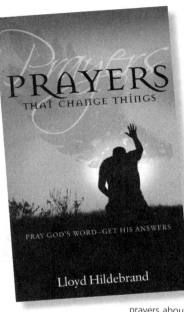

*P*rayers That Change Things is a new book by an established writer of books on prayer, Lloyd B. Hildebrand, who co-authored the very popular *Prayers That Prevail* series, *Bible Prayers for All Your Needs*, *Praying the Psalms*, *Healing Prayers*, and several others. This new book contains prayers about personal feelings and situations, prayers that are built directly from the Bible. The reader will discover that praying the Scriptures will truly bring about changes to so many things, especially their outlook on life and the circumstances of life. These life-imparting, life-generating, life-giving, and life-sustaining prayers are sure to bring God's answers to meet the believer's needs. Pray them from your heart; then wait for God to speak to you. Remember, He always speaks through His Word.

This revolutionary approach joins the power of prayer with the power of God's Word.

ISBN: 978-1-61036-105-7
MM / 192 pages

Bridge Logos